Walking Through The Seasons

A Living Archive of

Ceremony, Territory, and the Plants That Remember Us

By Darcy Fisher and Jenny Fisher

Keepers Of The Seasons, LLC

© 2025 Keepers Of The Seasons, LLC

All rights reserved. No part of this book may be reproduced or transmitted in any form by any means, electronic or mechanical, including photocopying and recording, or by any information storage and retrieval system, except as expressly permitted by the 1976 Copyright Act or by the publisher. Requests for permission and/or licensing should be made in writing to Keepers of The Seasons, LLC.

Keepers of The Seasons, LLC
P.O. Box 733
Arlee, MT 59821
www.sixtwenty.net
info@kotstek.com

Cover photo by Darcy Fisher
ISBN: 979-8-9938820-0-0

Disclaimer

The information in this book is not intended to diagnose, treat, cure, or prevent any disease and is not a substitute for professional medical advice. Readers are encouraged to consult qualified healthcare professionals for medical concerns

Who We Are

We're lifelong learners. Always dreaming.

We feel closest to home on the Pacific coast, even when we're far from it. Time on the road lets us wonder where the next chapter starts. We go off the regular roads, wander the mountains, take pictures. Not just for keepsakes. To share what we see.

We love comfort food. We love new foods. We love time with friends and family. Our daughter grounds us and gives us vision. She makes us ask: how do we make our future selves happy?

We dream of a bison farm. Sustainable ancestral diet. Making goods with our hands. More medicine. More gifts. More of what matters.

Our roots run through ʔamakis Ktunaxa and Salish, Kootenai, and Pend d'Oreille territories. The ancestral light shines through everything we make.

We hope to gift as much as we can. To those who matter. To those who will matter. To those who will receive what we leave when we're gone.

That's who we are. Still walking. Still dreaming. Still learning.

"Traditional Knowledge, Values and Skills are Important to preserving and sustaining our Cultural way of life".

Contents

How to Use This Book	10
Acknowledgements	13
Part One: The Foundation	17
Part Two: Learning to See	29
Serrated Leaves	39
Oblong Leaves	40
Ribbed or Rigid Leaves	43
Underground Treasures	44
Roots	47
ʔa·knumu¢ti‡i‡ (Natural Law and Order)	58
Part Three: Walking Through The Seasoons	62
Our Stories	74
Ka papa	79
Part Four: Spring	87
Kanuhus ʔa·knuq̓yuk̓ naʔuti	96
ʔa·kuwa‡wuʔk, Birch Tree/Paper Birch (Betula papyrifera)	100
kanu‡maqu‡aqpiʔk, Cottonwood (Populus balsamifera)	103
waʔta, Spring Beauty (Claytonia lanceolata)	104
¢uq̓kuna, Stinging Nettle (Urtica dioica)	107
ʔa·q̓uku ka‡muxu, Woodland Strawberry (Fragaria virginiana)	108
qa‡ukp, Yellowbells (Fritillaria pudica)	111
ʔinq̓um, Skunk Cabbage (Lysichiton americanus)	112
Red Clover (Trifolium pratense)	115
Oxeye Daisy (Leucanthemum vulgare)	116
Mountain Lady's Slipper (Cypripedium montanum)	119
Fairy Slipper(Calypso bulbosa)	120
ʔa·knuq̓yuk̓, Violet (Viola spp)	123
Xapi, Camas (Camassia quamash)	124
ʔa‡‡a, Edible Horsehair (Bryoria fremontii)	127
Maxa, Glacier Lily (Erythronium grandiflorum)	128
k̓itq̓u‡ka‡maxaka, Dandelion (Taraxacum officinale)	131
Xa‡, Arrowleaf Balsamroot (Balsamorhiza sagittata)	132
Trillium (Trillium ovatum)	135
Naqam¢u, Bitterroot (Lewisia rediviva)	136
Large-flowered Triteleia (Triteleia grandiflora)	139

Wild Licorice (Glycyrrhiza lepidota)	140
Sticky Purple Geranium (Geranium viscosissimum)	143
ʔinqam, Prairie Crocus (Anemone patens)	144
Wiyu, Prickly Pear (Opuntia fragilis)	147
Part Five: Summer	148
Ka's ki'in numa	156
Black Medick (Medicago lupulina)	166
sq̇umu, Saskatoon berry (Amelanchier alnifolia)	169
Ka¢ɫaquɫaqpi·k, Thimbleberry (Rubus parviflorus)	170
kitq̇uɫkaɫmaxaka, Yarrow (Achillea millefolium)	173
Kyanɫakɫiquɫaqpik, Heart-leafed Arnica (Arnica cordifolia)	174
Muk, Bunchberry (Cornus canadensis)	177
Quɫwa, Wood's Rose: petals (Rosa woodsii)	178
Yuk, Elderberry (Sambucus cerulea)	181
¢aqawuʔk, Kinnikinnick (Arctostaphylos uva-ursi)	182
ʔa·kɫaɫku, Bear-grass (Xerophyllum tenax)	185
Northern Bedstraw (Galium boreale)	186
Long-flowered Bluebells (Mertensia longiflora)	189
Comfrey (Symphytum officinale)	190
ʔa·knuqɫuxunaʔtit mata, Wild Bergamot (Monarda fistulosa)	193
Pink Wintergreen, Mata, (Pyrola asarifolia)	194
ɫawiyaɫ, Huckleberry (Vaccinium species)	197
kwiɫq̇a taq̇xaka, Common Burdock (Arctium minus)	198
Prairie Coneflower, Ratibida columnifera	201
ʔakinmiɫyukquɫaqpi·k, Labrador Tea (Rhododendron columbianum)	202
naqpumsaɫ, Fireweed (Epilobium angustifolium)	205
Mata, Self Heal (Prunella vulgaris)	206
Mata, Anise Hyssop (Agastache foeniculum)	209
Nasayit, Wood Lily (Lily philadelphicum)	210
niʔ¢na, Wild Carrot (Daucus carota)	213
ʔakuwaɫ, Wild Onion (Allium cernuum)	214
ʔakukaʔɫak, Nine-leaf Biscuitroot (Lomatium triternatum)	217
napknuququɫ, Desert Parsley (Lomatium sp.)	218
ʔanaʔnam, Pineapple Weed (Matricaria discoidea)	221
Curly-cup Gumweed, (Grindelia squarrosa)	222
ku¢uku, Pearly Everlasting (Anaphalis margaritacea)	225

Chicory, (Cichorium intybus)	226
skinku¢ yaqitis, Wild Tarragon (Artemisia dracunculus)	229
Goldenrod (Solidago canadensis)	230
Elk Thistle (Cirsium scariosum)	233
Great Mullein, kipiǂkukaka?muǂ, (Verbascum thapsus)	234
?a·ki?ǂmak, Chokecherry (Prunus virginiana)	237
Part Six: Fall	**238**
qanǂatana, Whitebark Pine (Pinus Albicaulis)	255
?akukpǂuǂaǂ, Rocky Mountain Juniper (Juniperus scopulorum)	256
?i¢hat, Western Red Cedar (Thuja plicata)	259
?aquǂaqpi·s, Creeping Dogbane (Apocynum cannabinum)	260
naǂi·¢axawu?k, Devil's Club (Oplopanax horridus)	263
?ayut, Bear Root (Ligusticum porteri)	264
Evergreen Needles, ?a·kuǂaǂ and Tree Resin, ?iǂwas	267
The Medicine Begins: Teas, Tonics, & Elixirs of the Seasons	270
Part Seven: Winter	**282**
Epilogue: The Long Handshake	**289**
References	295
Section 1 — Primary Sources & Teachings	296
Section 2 — Verification Sources by Plant	297
Section 3 — Plant-Specific Verification Sources	300
Section 4 — Additional Web Resources Consulted	311
GLOSSARY	312
About the Authors	317

How to Use This Book

About Language

Ktunaxa and Salish language appear throughout these pages where they serves the teaching. We take an observational approach. Sharing what we've witnessed, what we've learned, what the plants and knowledge holders have shown us. The language is here because it's true to that experience.

When we reference our ancestral language, we're speaking of the first languages we knew, the languages tied to specific places and peoples.

Your ancestors had languages too. Words shaped by the land they lived on, the plants they gathered, the relationships they tended. Those languages carry observation, relationship, and truth.

All of these languages, including the ones we've forgotten, point toward the same knowing: that love is the first language, and the land teaches it to everyone who listens.

This is not a language book. This is not a plant book. This is not limited to any one people or tradition.

This book is for anyone seeking relationship with the land, with themselves, with their potential. We share our lived experience. What we observed. What helped us grow. What transformed us, so that others might find their own path forward.

About Plant Profiles

You'll notice that plant profiles include Ktunaxa names alongside common and scientific names. Just as other plant guides use Latin binomials for precision, we use ancestral names because they carry specific understanding about relationship with these plants.

But this is not a field guide.

Each plant profile is an invitation to transformation. The plants teach us how to be human. How to heal, how to grow, how to reach our potential across all four quadrants: **physical, mental, emotional, spiritual.**

We're not teaching plant identification. We're sharing how plants became our teachers, and how that relationship can serve your personal growth, wherever you are, whoever you are.

Acknowledgements

We would like to start by giving thanks to our family and supporters who encouraged us to keep doing what we are doing. It is with gratitude, patience, and great humility that we took the time to create this book and share our knowledge and intergenerational teachings. We understand that we are gifted and that it is our duty to ensure our knowledge and message continues long after we are gone.

As with tradition, we thank Creator, our ancestors and the many generous knowledge holders who have shared their teachings along our life journey. Their wisdom has guided our path and deepened our connection to all living things (ʔa·kxamis q̓api qapsin').

Importantly, we thank our children for bringing us happiness, love, and reminding us about the importance of family. Watching them grow and connect with the land has been one of our greatest teachers. We also give thanks to the countless students who have been encouraged by the things we do and carry our teachings to their friends, families, and communities. Their enthusiasm keeps this knowledge alive and vibrant.

We give special thanks to our family members whose earth walk ended before the completion of our book, notably our Father, David Williams, and our t̓úpyeʔ, Genevieve 'Jenny' Matt. May we be fortunate enough to hear their songs, feel their guidance, and see them dance in the wind on the mountain tops.

We also want to thank the land (ʔamak) that has provided for us, and the plants that continue to offer their gifts. As we share this knowledge, we hope to inspire a deeper connection to the natural world and a commitment to preserving these traditional ways.

—Darcy and Jenny Fisher

Grandma's Love

My fondest memories of you, is your beautiful smile, laughter, thoughtfulness, and warm embrace, you had the best hugs.
I will remember always of your love, kindness, gentleness, intelligence, and beauty.
Of your observant nature, generosity and of how brave, strong, and hardworking and adventurous you were. You weren't afraid to be yourself and that's what I loved about you most of all.
Grandma you were the rock always there for all of us, no matter what, without judgment, giving freely your loving advice, always having a moment to lend a listening ear and prayers for everyone, especially those in need near and far.
Grams you had the best stories, of the old days and the many changes that you had seen. You shared of the mistakes made and hardships that you faced, of the good times and bad and how they shaped you to be the strong independent woman that we all knew.
The things you liked to share most of all was how proud you were of your children, grandchildren, great grandchildren, and of course extended family, and friends, happy for all their accomplishments, and life adventures and growth as a person.
As a child grandma you helped to instill in me imagination and wonderment of the world, as I grow older it was the importance of family, tradition, culture and most importantly being me.
Having self love, being happy and grateful for each day no matter how hard it may seem, or how hard the fall to get back up, dust yourself off, try again, and to never give up.
I will cherish the memories of the time spent and hold you near and dear in my heart always.
I am forever grateful that I am a part of you, and you will always be a part of me.
When I need you most, I know that you won't be far, that you will always be there to listen, and when I need guidance most, I am sure you will be right by my side supporting and loving me the whole time.
When I am lonely for you, I will look to nature, that is where I will be reminded of you most.
There I will sit and listen closely to the rivers, streams, creeks, springs, and there is where I hope to hear your voice and laughter.
When I am out and about in these places of wonderment, that is where I hope to hear your songs, in the winds that blow through the trees, grasses and mountain tops.
For you are my grandmother and your love is unconditional.

Written in memory of my beautiful grandmother
Genevieve Teresa Matt
— Jenny Fisher

"Where our ancestors sing in the wind and offer their guidance".
Hu‡ ȼina‡ ʔupna‡a titi / papa.

Part One: The Foundation

Introduction

In our hearts we have always known the plants speak. Not as metaphor, but as daily truth. The way cedar calls you home before you even smell it, the way bitterroot shows you exactly where to dig, the way cottonwood whispers which direction the weather's turning.

Our connection to Mother Earth runs deep in our bloodline like water through stone. Carved by countless generations who understood that we are not separate from the land but woven together. Our ancestors made a covenant with Creator; to serve our families. Serving as stewards, honoring our connection, and remembering that survival means relationship.

This isn't another plant guide. This is a remembering.

We offer this book as a path back to what was never truly lost: connection to land, our loved ones, and ourselves. This book is for those who feel something stirring when their hands touch the earth. For the ones whose gifts have been called disorders; when they were always medicine. For anyone who senses there's another way: one that is quieter, older, rooted in relation.

How the Plants Taught Us to Listen

The language of the plants *(ʔa·kłukaqwum)* doesn't come through words. It moves through your whole being, a scent that changes your breathing, a texture that teaches your fingers, colors that wake memories.

We learned to receive this communication the way our grandmothers, great-grandmothers, and ancestors did: by slowing down and paying attention, trusting our bodies. Our intuition. Our truth.

Our elders didn't hand us this knowledge in an afternoon. They walked us through seasons. Showed us what changes, what stays constant, what we miss when we're moving too fast. The plants correct you gently at first: bitter taste, wrong timing, empty basket, roots that break when you pull too hard. Then more firmly if you don't listen.

The plants can feel the difference between genuine attention and wishful projection. They respond to sincerity, patience, and the willingness to be corrected when we misunderstand.

Sweet smells that call you closer. Thorns that teach respect. Roots that show you how to go deep when the surface gets harsh.

The plants have been trying to teach us all along. **We just forgot how to be good students.**

The Remembering: How We Live it Now

Our ancestors lived by principles that kept the world in balance. These weren't rules imposed from outside. They were relationships discovered through generations of listening and observing:

Gratitude: We give thanks daily for life. For the simple moments. The precious moments. The shared experiences.

Integrity: Following through on what we promise. Especially when no one's watching.

Reciprocity: Taking only what we need. Leaving the rest. Offering tobacco, song, something of personal value. Our ancestors understood: life is a gift. And we're just learning to give back.

Protocol: Setting our intention through heart-mind connection. Harvesting when the plant is ready, not when we are. Leaving the land the same or better than we found it.

Humility: Staying humble enough to know when we're wrong. Remaining students for life. The plants have been here longer than we have. They know things we're still learning.

What We've Learned Walking This Path

Connection is relationship. Relationship of spirit, of heart, of mind, of all living things. This is what many Indigenous peoples have always known.

When others speak of the natural world using terms like "biophysical components," they're trying to make sense of relationships that can't be separated without breaking them. We understand their intent, but these words cannot hold what we know to be true.

We don't speak of components. We speak of the whole being. The land and water are living, interconnected, and inseparable from spirit, ceremony, and the wellness of all beings.

When we approach plant teachings, seasonal protocols, or healing relationships, we consider not only what appears on the surface, but the cultural, spiritual, and intergenerational connections that weave through everything.

This wholeness is what our plant teachers have shown us. This is why our children's sensitivity isn't too much. It's the same awareness that helped our ancestors tend these relationships with the land and living world for thousands of years.

This understanding guides everything we share. **It's the foundation our medicine rests on.**

Our children are the most beautiful whole beings we will ever meet, and it is our privilege to nurture them in ways that keep their spirits intact. To feed them not only with food and water, but with love, story, and belonging.

And for those still learning how to receive such care, know this: the heart remembers. It knows the way home, to laughter, to love, to the belonging you've always deserved.

You, the one reading, feeling something stir, this is your invitation to return. You were never broken, only waiting to be loved back into wholeness.

Wholeness as the First Teaching

Through our learning, we've come to understand that plants offer themselves in four sacred ways. Each revealing a facet of the wholeness that lives within all things.

Food (xapi, sq̓umu, ɬawiyaɬ): Plants that nourish our bodies and remind us to eat in rhythm with the turning of the seasons. In their generosity, they teach that nourishment is not consumption; it is relationship. Each bite, each sip, an act of gratitude.

Medicine (ʔawumu): Plants that ease pain and restore balance. Their medicine extends beyond the body, healing the distance between self and world.

Tools: Plants that shelter, clothe, warm, and carry. They teach that usefulness can be graceful, and that creation begins with respect. When we shape what they offer, we remember that our hands are part of the earth's work.

Spirit: Plants carried in ceremony by those who hold specific medicine. They speak to the parts of us beyond words, reminding us that Spirit moves quietly through all things, unseen but never absent.

Many plants carry all four gifts. *Just like people.*

Each of us carries the ability to feed, heal, create, and guide. These are not separate callings, but the movements of one whole being remembering itself.

Wholeness is not a lesson to be learned. It is the memory that stirs when we stop running from ourselves.

It is what waits beneath the noise of striving. Beneath every grief. Beneath every joy.

It is the pulse of life that has never left us. And when we begin to live from that place, the ground feels nearer, the breath comes easier, and the world itself seems to lean closer, listening to the sound of us remembering who we are.

To live whole is to walk as prayer.

To love, to make, to tend, to give. These are the ways we remember.

What This Book Is and Isn't

We trained with knowledge holders who taught us not just what to harvest, but **how to be in relationship** with what we harvest.

We've woven these plant relatives into our own lives. Our healing, our daily ceremony of eating, breathing, and remembering who we are.

We share our stories not as prescriptions, but as pathways. We're not doctors in the Western sense. **We are relatives**, sharing what helped our family remember something important about the gifts that live in relationship with the natural world (*ʔa·kxamis q̓api qapsin'*).

This book won't diagnose, treat, or cure anything in the way institutions understand those words.

But it might help you remember capacities you thought you'd lost. It might help you see that **what you call broken may actually be medicine trying to emerge.**

We've learned to speak both languages. The language of ceremony and the language institutions understand. **We use both to serve the medicine.**

For the Ones Ready to Remember

If you've made it this far, something in you already knows. Maybe it's the part of you that stops to touch bark when no one's looking. Maybe it's the voice that whispers the names of plants you don't remember learning. Maybe it's the quiet recognition that your sensitivity isn't too much.

This book is ceremony. A way of walking that honors the old agreements while meeting the world as it is. It is a bridge between the knowledge that never left and the humans ready to receive it again.

The plants are still speaking. They've been waiting for us to remember how to listen. And when you're ready to hear them, something shifts.

Remembering the Gatherer

There comes a moment. Often in parenthood. Sometimes before. When the covenant becomes real. Not a story told by elders, but a living weight you feel in your chest, your hands, your decisions.

You become the gatherer.

Not because you chose it, but because something ancient within you awakened and said: *It's time. The ones who came before are watching. The ones yet to come are waiting. You are the bridge.*

The ancestors speak through memory that lives in the body. Suddenly you remember: being small, barefoot, hands reaching for plants whose names you hadn't learned but somehow knew.

These aren't just memories. They're instructions.

When you slow down. When you pay attention. When you trust what your body already knows; the ancestors' messages become unmistakable:

The scent of cedar is remembering.
The hum of bees is teaching.
The rhythm of hands making food is ceremony.
The calling of plants by name is relationship.

You start piecing it together. Fragments your grandmothers shared, dreams that felt too real, the way certain places make your bones hum, how you just *know* things about plants before anyone teaches you.

This is attunement. Connecting the pieces our ancestors knew, recognizing they planted these knowings in us before we were born.

The gatherer role isn't new. It's ancient. It's the one who:

- Provides (not just food, but medicine, beauty, ceremony)
- Protects (through wisdom, protocol, relationship)
- Remembers (carries forward what cannot be lost)
- Teaches (passes the covenant to those yet to come)

And now it's you.

Maybe it awakened with your first child. The fierce knowing that you must create a home filled with jars of food and medicine, teach them what grandmothers taught, show them they're part of creation's breath.

Maybe it awakened when you held seeds passed down through generations and understood: *These aren't just seeds. They're promises. And I'm being asked to keep them.*

Maybe it awakened standing in a place your ancestors walked, feeling their presence so strong you couldn't deny it anymore.

However it came, you felt it: The gatherer rising within you.

Not as burden, but as homecoming.

Not as loss of self, but as remembering who you always were.

This is why we walk through the seasons. Not to learn something new, but to remember what we already carry. To honor the covenant our ancestors made. To gather not just plants, but the scattered pieces of ourselves. To become whole enough to pass the knowledge forward.

Great-grandmothers' gardens are still growing in the soil of memory.

You are the child with hands full of flowers.
You are the one returning them in gratitude.
You are the covenant continuing.

The ancestors speak. We attune. The gathering continues.

Part Two: Learning to See

Identification: Learning the Language of Plants

You'll see plants identified by their common names, scientific names, and Ktunaxa names. The names are doorways. What matters is the relationship you build once you step through.

Before we speak of identification, we must speak of **relationship**. Our ancestors understood that learning to recognize plants was not merely about information; it was about **developing the capacity to receive communication** from the living world.

When children learned plant names, they were learning **how to be human in a way that serves life**.

> *"To name a plant is to begin a conversation that can last a lifetime."*

As we continue our journey through the seasons, we come to understand that identifying plants is a **conversation**. One that requires our whole being:
our eyes to see patterns, our hands to feel textures, and our hearts to receive the deeper teachings that each plant carries.

True identification begins when we slow down enough to recognize that **knowing a plant's name is only the first step.** Listening is what turns knowledge into relationship.

Ways We Come to Know Plants

Before we can identify a plant, we must first **acknowledge the many ways of knowing** that live within us.

Our ancestors never separated learning from relationship; they understood that the mind, body, and spirit all take part in recognition. Each person receives information through different pathways. Some through sight, some through scent or touch, others through intuition and feeling. All are valid. All are needed.

To learn plants is to remember how to listen with the whole self. Some people notice pattern and color before form; others sense energy or hear the whisper of movement in the wind. What often gets labeled as distraction is actually attunement. The ability to notice multiple forms of communication at once.

Honoring All Ways of Knowing

We spoke of our children as the most beautiful whole beings we will ever meet. This truth extends to all learners.

Each person carries their own experience of how their ways of knowing were received. These experiences shape how we show up, how we learn, how we trust ourselves.

How do we keep wholeness intact? How do we honor all ways of knowing? How do we validate experience while nurturing growth?

Attunement and validation go hand in hand. To truly understand and nurture all ways of knowing, we must first know ourselves. To know what validation looks like. To know when our experience has been positive and helps us flourish. To remember the light that went off when we reframed our thoughts. When space for growth and positive change was provided. We were finally able to free ourselves from things that were never meant for us to carry. This space and realization puts us on the journey of self-actualization. Of knowing and showing our true self. Of trusting our instinct. Of seeing and embodying our wholeness.

Learning how we show up in the world becomes the practice. How our experiences shape our responses. How our thoughts create our reality. How our awareness expands our capacity.

We learn that we cannot be broken. Our wholeness remains. Waiting to be remembered. Waiting to be reclaimed.

This type of life-changing experience helps us map where we have been, where we are, and where we are going. We welcome positive change. We face challenges. We achieve milestones. Our limits. Our potential. What we've achieved that can never be taken away.

Self-work isn't optional. It's how we build capacity for relationship. When we name what shows up: anger, grief, joy, overwhelm, curiosity, we build relationship with all parts of ourselves. Not as excuses, but as understanding.

Through this practice, we can walk in another's shoes. Feeling what they feel. Recognizing what gets carried. Not to fix, but to be present with.

We lead with empathy. Heart to heart. Spirit to spirit work. This is how we walk with the plants. This is how we teach. This is how we honor all ways of knowing.

Deepening Through the Senses

When we do the work of knowing ourselves, of honoring our wholeness, we begin to trust our senses again. We learn to rely on what our eyes see, what our hands feel, what our nose recognizes before our mind names it.

This is how self-work deepens our relationship with plants. The more whole we become, the more we can receive. Visual cues. Scent. Taste. Touch. Each sense becomes a doorway into deeper knowing.

Our ancestors understood this. They didn't separate self-knowledge from plant knowledge. To know yourself was to know how you

receive information from the living world. To trust your instincts was to trust what the plants were teaching.

The following pathways: visual, sensory, seasonal, are not just methods of identification. They are practices of deepening relationship. With plants. With land. With the wholeness that lives in all things.

Visual Recognition

Sometimes it's just a way to be.

Present.

With what your eyes are drawn to.

Notice the vibrant colors of flowers. The unique arrangements of inflorescence. How they speak of identity, family, purpose.

Notice whether trees are coniferous or deciduous. How their nature and lifecycle teach adaptation and resilience.

Notice the distinctive patterns, textures, and hues that make each plant unique.

There's no rush. No test. Just presence with what you see.

Sensory Learning

Plants speak through all our senses, not just sight.

Touch: the feeling of leaves, the grain of bark, the weight of roots in your hands.

Smell: the scent that reveals a plant before your eyes do.

Sound: how wind moves through different leaves, how seed pods rattle when ready.

Intuition: the quiet knowing that comes when you are still enough to receive it.

All of these are ways of being with plants. Not studying them. Being with them.

Walking Through the Seasons

To walk through the seasons is to apprentice yourself to time as the land keeps it. Each bud, flower, seed, and shadow tells a part of the story.

When we follow plants through their cycles, we begin to understand that growth and rest are not opposites, but kin. Every emergence, bloom, and decay is a lesson in timing and reciprocity.

To know a plant in spring is to know only one chapter of its story. To return in summer, autumn, and winter; to watch it leaf, fruit, wither, and sleep is to learn its language. Through this slow witnessing, we become participants rather than collectors. The land begins to recognize us in return.

This teaches patience, humility, and continuity. It reminds us that our senses are instruments of study and of prayer. The gleam on a new leaf, the scent of sap rising, the sound of seed pods cracking open, all are messages in the world's ongoing conversation.

When we walk through the seasons with awareness, we learn that the plants are never still. They turn with the sun, respond to touch, reach for water, and rest when it is time to rest. And in learning their pace, we remember our own.

The Relationship Cycle

Harvesting is a sacred act rooted in the principles of ʔa·knumu¢titiⱡ, Natural Law and Order. It is not a single moment of taking, but part of an ongoing cycle of relationship, learning, and reciprocity.

This cycle unfolds in three living phases, each mirroring how life itself gives and receives:

Pre-Harvest Preparation: Before we ever touch a plant, we prepare ourselves spiritually and mentally. We offer gratitude to the Creator, our ancestors, and the plant nations for sharing their wisdom. We set our intention with a good heart and ask permission to gather. This preparation reminds us that we are entering into a sacred relationship, not initiating a transaction.

Mindful Harvesting: With permission granted, we observe the plant community closely, listening for signs that individuals are ready to offer their medicine. We take only what is needed, leaving enough for regeneration and for the other beings who depend on it. Offerings of tobacco, song, or breath are given in return, acknowledging that the plant's gift is freely given, not owed. Through this exchange, we learn that harvesting is a conversation, not an act of possession.

Reciprocity: After the harvest, our relationship continues. We process and store the medicine with care, thanking it for its healing power. We give back in tangible ways: returning seeds, tending the soil, removing harm, or sharing the teachings that emerged from the experience.

When we walk in this way, with humility, integrity, and reciprocity, we remember our place in the web of life. We recognize that plants are not resources, but relations, each with their own purpose, presence, and wisdom.

Through this continuous cycle we come to understand that our health and the land's health are one story. Every season, every harvest, is another verse in that story. A reminder that relationship itself is the medicine. That healing is the result of an ongoing

committed response to balance and care.

Seasonal Protocols: Learning Natural Law

There are specific protocols for harvesting different plant parts that honor ʔa·knumu¢tiłił, Natural Law and Order. Through these practices, we remember: when we care for the land, the land cares for us.

ʔayut (Bear Root): We harvest Bear Root only in cooler seasons, when the plant's energy has withdrawn into its roots. By not gathering during its flowering time, we respect its reproductive cycle. This practice teaches energy awareness and timing, lessons equally vital for human balance and restraint.

Bark Collection: When gathering bark, we take only thin, vertical strips when the tree's sap is low, and never girdle the trunk. This demonstrates how to take what we need without causing harm, a law that extends to all forms of relationship.

When we honor these protocols, we participate in a cycle that keeps both land and spirit in balance.

Learning to See: Plant Identification Features

Leaf Arrangement: Alternate, opposite, whorled, or basal.

Leaf Shape and Margin: Lobed, toothed, or smooth-edged. Pointed or rounded at the tip.

Flowers: Color, number, and arrangement of petals and sepals.

Fruits and Seeds: Berry, drupe, capsule. How seeds disperse: wind, water, or animal.

Bark, Buds, and Stems: Texture, color, growth habit.

The following pages offer detailed features to deepen your observation. Space is provided for your own notes and reflections.

Pa·quku/kaɫmuxu
Wild Strawberry (Fragaria virginiana)

Serrated Leaves

Serrated leaves are common in the **Rosaceae** family, marked by the distinctive ridges or *"teeth"* along their edges.
These serrations are often more pronounced near the top of the leaf and gradually smooth toward the base.

Examples:

- Huckleberry (ɫawiyaɫ)
- Roses (q̇uɫwa)
- Service/Saskatoon berry (sq̇umu)
- Wild Strawberry (ʔa·q̇uku / kaɫmuxu)

Journey Notes and Personal Reflections

___
___
___
___
___
___
___
___
___
___
___
___
___
___
___
___
___
___
___
___
___
___
___
___
___
___

Oblong Leaves

Oblong leaves are smooth-edged, often without serrations, and have a soft, even texture to the touch.

This is one of the most common leaf shapes in nature, found across many plant families and ecosystems.

Examples:

- Labrador Tea (High Mountain tea - ʔakinmiɬyukquɬaqpi·k)
- Willow (ɬam̓)
- Foamberry (Soopolallie - kupaʔtiɬ)

Journey Notes and Personal Reflections

_____
_____
_____
_____
_____
_____
_____
_____
_____
_____
_____
_____
_____
_____
_____
_____
_____
_____
_____
_____
_____
_____

Paʼkutwuʔk/ naʔmaʼ
Green Alder (Alnus viridis)

Ribbed or Rigid Leaves

Ribbed or rigid leaves are defined by their pronounced veins and a firm, structured texture when touched.

Examples:

- Red osier dogwood (mukwuʔk)
- Bunchberry
- Alder (ʔakuɫwuʔk)

Journey Notes and Personal Reflections

_____
_____
_____
_____
_____
_____
_____
_____
_____
_____
_____
_____
_____
_____
_____
_____
_____
_____
_____
_____
_____
_____
_____

Underground Treasures

Many ancestral food and medicine plants store their strength and nourishment underground.

Bulbs

Bulbs are compact vessels that contain the full potential of the plant until it emerges in its season.

Examples:
- Spring beauty/Indian Potato (waʔta)
- Camas (xapi)
- Nodding Onion (ʔakuwaɫ)

Journey Notes and Personal Reflections

Western Spring Beauty (Claytonia lanceolata)

Roots

Our ancestors valued roots for their medicinal properties, natural dyes, and as nutrient-dense sources of carbohydrates, vitamins, and minerals.

Examples:

- Arrow leaf balsamroot (xaɫ)
- Bitterroot (naqam¢u)
- Dandelion (k̓itq̓uɬkaɬmaxaka)

Journey Notes and Personal Reflections

_____
_____
_____
_____
_____
_____
_____
_____
_____
_____
_____
_____
_____
_____
_____
_____
_____
_____
_____
_____
_____
_____
_____
_____
_____
_____

When Plants Speak: Spiritual Guidance and Barriers

Understanding how plants communicate is a matter of attention and relationship. Traditional language names not just what exists, but how it relates.

When identifying plants for traditional or ancestral harvest, we are often guided spiritually. Through dreams, intuition, or direction from knowledge keepers.

Historically, those called to become medicine people entered long apprenticeships of fasting, ceremony, and vision quests, living in direct reciprocity with the natural world. Their learning was relational training. Becoming attuned to scent, texture, sensation. Learning to recognize what dreams were teaching. Trusting what their bodies felt in the presence of certain plants.

Knowing how plant shapes mirrored the body itself. Mullein, straight and erect, resembling our central nervous system: spine, back, pathways to the brain. Yellow dock mimicking blood platelets. Milkweed reflecting the liver. The natural world shows us what heals what.

Our ancestors taught that plants communicate through sensation, rhythm, and relationship rather than words. They move through us as scent, texture, and vibration. Lessons carried through experience rather than speech. This capacity develops through time and relationship.

Elders taught us to test what we think we hear. To seek community guidance, observe results, and stay humble enough to be corrected. The plants can feel sincerity. They respond to patience, to attention, and to the courage it takes to listen beyond certainty.

Sweet smells that call you closer. Thorns that teach respect. Roots that show you how to go deep when the surface gets harsh. The plants have been trying to teach us all along. We just forgot how to be good students.

What Gets in the Way

The ability to hear plants doesn't disappear. But sometimes we disconnect.

Our spirit can fragment from our actual existence. Anxiety. Depression. Dissociation. We stop recognizing life as life. We become numb to what's around us.

These barriers are real. They limit our experience. But they also give us the chance to grow. To reconnect. To return.

This is part of the cycle. Disconnection happens. What matters is

the return.

When faced with these barriers, we come back to foundational practices. Spending time with plants. Quieting the noise. Trusting what we feel. Remembering our place within the community of life. Maintaining reciprocity. Employing heart-mind integration.

The ability is still there. It's just waiting for us to return.

Children as Teachers

Children are born with memory, with knowing. They come into the world already carrying old understanding. It speaks through their curiosity, their stillness, and the way they greet the land as if it has been waiting just for them.

Watching young ones gather plants reveals this truth. A three-year-old finding bitterroot without being shown where to look. Small hands digging with natural grace, then holding it gently. The memory lives in their bones, passed down through bloodlines even when we forget.

Young children move carefully around plants, aware not to step on them. When sweetgrass brushes their hand, they might say "I'm sorry, I love you" or kiss it. They understand relationship naturally. Not because they were taught, but because they haven't learned to disconnect yet.

Children are aware of feeling. How all living beings can be treated with respect and dignity. When something brings light, happiness, comfort, balance into their space, they honor it. Unconditional.

Witnessing their purity, their wholeness, can bring tears. Not tears of self-pity, but something deeper. Our heart remembering. Being touched by Creator. Finally softening enough to let it in.

For some, these tears come because a memory returned. Twenty years later, or a lifetime. For survivors who've been running: through work, through relationships, through anything that kept attention away from connection. Then circumstances change. Loss of loved ones. Unclosed chapters. Closed chapters. Cancer. Cognitive decline. The moments that break us open, that stop us from saying "I'll work on it when I have time."

We don't set the clock. We chase it, always. Until we can't anymore.

Witnessing children's wholeness cracks us open. Makes us safe enough to finally feel what we've been running from. To remember what was taken. To grieve. To let love flow again: to family, to ourselves, to the work we're called to do. To let the light of a new day in.

Children show us how to stop chasing that clock. How to be present.

Now. Wholeness isn't something to achieve later. It's already here. Not to own. Not to mold. Not to make perfect. It already is.

Every precious moment brings light to our soul. Heals deep wounds. Allows us to forgive. To grow. To flourish. To become light, love, and laughter ourselves.

Children show us that love is the first language. That memory is born with us. That the earth remembers us through our children. Being a parent is not about teaching. It's about witnessing. Children remind us to walk gently, love fiercely, and find wonder in the smallest things.

Through them, we know the future is already remembering its way home.

When Gifts Get Called Disorders

We spoke earlier about honoring all ways of knowing. Here's where that teaching meets the systems that pathologize difference.

The effects of separation show up in many ways: grief, illness, disconnection, and even how our attention moves. What some systems call "disorder," our ancestors recognized as spirit and body trying to find their way back to balance.

This is cultural teaching, not medical advice. If you or someone you love has been diagnosed with ADHD, autism spectrum, or sensory processing differences, continue working with qualified healthcare providers. What we offer here is an additional framework, not a replacement.

What modern systems call "ADHD" or "sensory processing differences" often includes enhanced pattern recognition, environmental sensitivity, and intuitive awareness. Exactly the capacities our ancestors used for plant identification and ecological relationship.

What We've Witnessed

When people, especially those with heightened sensitivity, spend regular time in natural environments:

Their "distractibility" becomes an asset. They notice what others overlook.

Their "impulsivity" reveals itself as rapid, intuitive responsiveness.

Their "difficulty with focus" dissolves when learning or doing has real meaning.

Their "sensory overload" eases in organic sound, scent, and movement instead of artificial stimulation.

We're not claiming this is universal. We're sharing what we've seen, repeatedly, in our own family and community.

Beyond Children: A Universal Calling

There is strength in the universal approach, because this is not only about children. It's about all of us. It's for those who see the systems that have failed them and their loved ones, and refuse to remain bystanders while the next generation is molded into obedient compliance or quietly forgotten.

This is a place to call your own spirit home. To nurture the inner child. To remember empathy for minds and bodies that learn and absorb differently. **To stay attuned, to not allow your spirit to be dulled or severed from the whole being.**

Much like the plants, we are not meant to be compartmentalized. We are relational beings, always communicating through pattern, rhythm, and resonance. When we tend that connection, we begin to remember what the land has been saying all along: **sensitivity is not fragility. It's a way of knowing.**

And when we remember this, when we begin to see our own sensitivity, grief, and tenderness as intelligence, then the healing work extends far beyond the individual. It becomes collective remembering. It becomes ceremony. It becomes the way home.

Supporting Development Through Ancestral Lens

Traditional education in our communities cultivated intelligence through eco-immersion: learning directly from the living systems that sustain us.

This way of teaching did not separate body from mind, or learner from land. It recognized that every being carries a distinct way of perceiving, and that diversity of perception keeps communities healthy and adaptable.

Learning was never confined to age or ability. It was a lifelong journey guided by observation, participation, and story. The natural world itself was the classroom, and every learner had a place within it.

- Immersion in natural environments, where sensitivity became strength
- Experiential, hands-on learning that grounds knowledge in tangible relevance
- Respect for individual timing, without arbitrary age-based milestones
- Connection to lineage and purpose, creating intrinsic motivation

This way of teaching recognized that learning happens in rhythm with relationship.

When people spend time in nature, they don't simply study. They remember.

They learn through touch, scent, repetition, and reciprocity. A process of eco-immersion that activates body, heart, and mind as one awareness.

Eco-Immersion

Eco-immersion is not a new idea. It is the contemporary language for what our ancestors already practiced.

Traditional determinants of health included rites of passage, ceremony, fasting, vision quest, naming, kinship responsibilities, and purpose. Each practice cultivated spiritual, mental, emotional, and physical balance, ensuring that a person remained in right relationship with self, family, land, and spirit.

Eco-immersion continues this lineage of balance.

It invites us to remember that **healing and learning were never separate. They are the same ceremony of belonging.**

To live immersed in the land is to participate in a living system of education where the body becomes the classroom, the seasons the curriculum, and reciprocity the final assessment. Through this return, we reawaken the ancient truth that knowledge is not stored in books or buildings alone. It is breathed, sung, and remembered through relationship.

Eco-immersion is both ancestral and revolutionary.

It restores continuity between the old and the new, reminding us that connection itself is medicine. When we re-enter this living dialogue with the natural world, we begin to mend what was forgotten: reuniting mind with body, body with land, and knowledge with purpose.

Knowing, however, is only the first step. Living it is the ceremony that follows.

This is where integrity takes form: in the small, daily acts that align our thoughts, choices, and movements with care for all living things.

In the stillness between breaths, the self softens, and we remember our belonging to all that surrounds us.

ʔa·knumuȼtiɬiɬ (Natural Law and Order)

Our worldview is defined by oral history, stories, cultural traditions, and customs, all interwoven with the land. Through ancestral teachings and shared knowledge, we bring together past and present practices that remind us to embrace and celebrate our connection to all living things (*ʔa·kxaṁis q̓api qapsin'*).

"Each time we bring a new learner out on the land, we are ensuring and preserving generational footprints and connection to the land and all living things."

The Living Knowledge of the Land

Indigenous Ecological Knowledge (IEK) is generational science: knowledge of the land (*ʔamak*) that connects our stories to our evolutionary and resilient history. Our language (*ʔa·kɬukaqwum*) serves as both nomenclature and taxonomy of our surroundings; every word carries observation and truth.

In *Ktunaxa*, language describes relationship through lived experience:

- *ʔa·ka̓ɬakaʔis watak* — "Frog's bellybutton," our word for mushroom.
- *ʔa·kpiȼis ɬawu* — "Elk's (cow's) favorite food," our word for Pipsissewa.

Ethnobotany and learning the language of the plants are acts of cultural and linguistic preservation.

Guiding Principles of *ʔa·knumuȼtiɬiɬ*

Our guiding principles for responsible and respectful gathering are deeply rooted in *ʔa·knumuȼtiɬiɬ*. These are not abstract rules. **They are living expressions of relationship** with the land and all beings that share it. Each embodies thousands of years of observation, spiritual practice, and ecological ethics passed from generation to generation.

Gratitude

Gratitude begins before we ever take from the land. We give thanks to the Creator, our ancestors, and the teachers who carried this knowledge forward. We acknowledge the plants themselves for sharing their essence, recognizing that their gifts are not owed to us but freely given within a reciprocal relationship.

When we approach plants with gratitude, our perception changes. We become more attentive to their needs, more respectful of their cycles, and more aware of their teachings. Gratitude continues long after harvest, as we prepare, share, and use what was offered.

Integrity

Integrity means doing what is right even when no one is watching. It calls us to follow through on our intentions and responsibilities to the land and our community. **To harvest with integrity is to honor our covenant with the land.**

Integrity also shapes how we speak about our plant relationships: We do not exaggerate, appropriate, or claim knowledge beyond what we hold. When we make mistakes, as all learners do, we acknowledge them and learn.

Integrity lives in the quiet moments when our actions match our words, especially when our only witnesses are the plants themselves.

Reciprocity

Reciprocity teaches that relationship must be mutual. We take what we need and give in return: through tobacco, song, prayer, or action. This exchange recognizes that we are not taking, but participating in a cycle of giving.

To harvest with reciprocity is to ensure future abundance: sometimes by returning seeds, sometimes by tending habitat, and always by giving thanks.

Reciprocity sustains our people and the land alike. When we give back, we protect the future, ensuring that all who follow may also gather in balance and respect.

Protocol

Protocol guides how we approach and harvest plants. It begins with setting intention, a clear mind and a good heart, and asking spiritual permission before gathering. We harvest only when the time is right, taking care not to disturb more than is needed, and always leaving the land the same or better than we found it.

Protocols are not arbitrary; they are teachings refined through generations of practice and prayer. They teach when to harvest, which parts to use, how much to take, and who may gather certain medicines.

By following these protocols, we honor both the plants and the ancestral wisdom that sustains them.

Humility

Humility keeps us teachable. It is knowing when to listen, when to pause, and when to admit we are still learning. It asks us to approach plants not as resources, but as teachers.

In ethnobotany, humility reminds us that no single person holds all knowledge. The land has been teaching since time immemorial, and each of us receives only fragments of its wisdom.

When we remain humble, we notice the subtle signs: the way plants grow together, the timing of their flowering, the quiet conversations between species.

Humility also guides how we engage with other knowledge holders. We listen before speaking, observe before acting, and recognize that many paths of wisdom converge under Natural Law.

Carrying the Teachings Forward

Further to these principles, we uphold the importance of language and culture in maintaining our relationship with the land. Learning plant names, preparing medicines, and mentoring new learners are all acts of continuity, living expressions of care and reciprocity.

These teachings extend beyond harvesting; they are a way of being in relationship with all of life. When we embody gratitude, integrity, reciprocity, protocol, and humility, we cultivate right relationship not only with plants but with each other and the world that sustains us.

When we live by these teachings, we strengthen our capacity to embody them in all our relationships, ensuring that the covenant between people and land remains unbroken.

Journey Reflections

As you consider these principles that guide our relationship with plants and the land, you might reflect on your own journey:

- How do you express gratitude in your own life? When you gather food or medicine from the land, or even when you purchase plant products, how might you acknowledge their origins?

- Where do you find opportunities to practice integrity in your relationship with the natural world? What does it mean to "do the right thing even when no one is watching" in your own context?

- How might the concept of reciprocity change your approach to the plants you use? What gifts, tangible or intangible, can you offer in return for what you receive?

- What protocols guide your interactions with the world around you? How might developing personal practices and rituals deepen your connection to the plants in your region?

- When has humility opened you to new understanding? How might approaching plants as teachers rather than resources transform your relationship with them?

These questions aren't meant to have simple answers. They're invitations to journey deeper into your own connection with all living things, allowing these principles to grow from concepts into lived experience.

Walking Through the Seasons

"Each footprint we leave connects us to the past, grounds us in the present and guides us to the future; we learn to tread lightly and pace ourselves through mindfulness, intention and prayer."

Celebration and Preservation: Living the Old Ways

Our connection and the gifts we share become most visible during times of feast, gratitude, and celebration. The foods we prepare, the laughter that fills our homes, and the stories that move between generations remind us to honor life in all its cycles.

As young learners, we participated in many feasts, giveaways, and community gatherings, each one carrying lessons in generosity, gratitude, and humility. We tended fires, prepared food, fetched water, sat with elders, listened to stories. The whole act was ceremony. Now, as knowledge holders, we weave these same values into our yearly harvesting and preservation practices, ensuring the continuity of relationship through both ceremony and everyday life.

We learned traditional pit-cooking, drying, smoking, and preservation methods: teachings passed down through generations. Honoring what we were taught, we carry these customs forward into our own gatherings, keeping them alive.

Pit-Cooking Traditions

One of the most meaningful ways we prepare traditional foods is through pit-cooking: an earth-centered method that embodies patience and reverence. This process can be used for many foods and has long served as a ceremonial act of unity and nourishment.

We often prepare Camas (*xapi*), a traditional root food, alongside wild game. Pit-cooking uses indirect heat, similar to slow cooking, allowing the earth itself to share in the transformation. Camas requires extended cooking to break down the starches (inulin) into simpler sugars, turning bitterness into sweetness and complexity into sustenance.

In this slow, patient process, we remember that everything worth keeping takes time.

Honoring Abundance

When we are blessed with abundant harvests, we draw upon both traditional and contemporary preservation methods: drying, fermenting, smoking, and freezing, to ensure that no gift is wasted. Each method becomes a form of prayer: a gesture of respect, a song of gratitude, a promise to the generations who will follow.

To preserve is to remember. It is how we give thanks for what the land has offered and ensure that its generosity continues to nourish

the circle of life.

When we live these teachings, they take form in celebration, where harvest becomes ceremony, and knowledge becomes nourishment.

Learning from Our Children

These preservation practices become even more meaningful when we share them with the next generation. Bringing our youngest child out onto the land has been one of our greatest gifts. Being in the mountains with her since before she could walk has reminded us to see the world with the same wonderment our children do.

Watching her grow from no words to ancestral words for plants, and to observing the land closely enough to know what is almost in season, has been a deeply fulfilling experience. She has taught us to be mindful of what we say and how we say it, how we teach and how we learn.

Our daughter has rekindled memories of our earliest experiences with plants, especially those that are edible, memorable, and sometimes challenging. If it's edible, she's willing to try it, at least once.

We have many fond memories of first experiences with edible and medicinal plants. Some of the most memorable involved adults teaching through play and jokes. Soapberry/foamberry (*kupaʔtiɬ*) is a perfect example. Always ready to teach, they'd pop a handful of the bright red berries into their mouths, saying how good they were, then encourage us to do the same. The bitter and sour notes straight off the plant? Not pleasant. But mixed with other berries as "Indian ice cream"? Delicious.

Lessons worth learning can be done with patience, love, and playfulness. No heavy hand needed. We still encourage our daughter to try them each year, laughing as we remember.

Indigenous Connectedness and Mindfulness

Watching our daughter learn has reminded us that knowledge doesn't live in one place. It moves through all parts of our being. Through her eyes, we have remembered the teachings that shape how we learn: that knowledge begins in relationship and deepens through time. We are rooted and grounded in our connection to ancestral knowledge and all living things. Through introspection, Indigenous Connectedness teaches us who we are, where we come from, and the gifts we carry. It also reminds us to let go of past limitations to make space for positive change and renewal.

"Spiritual, Mental, Emotional, and Physical wellness can be influenced by our connection to the land."

Indigenous Connectedness through Mindfulness helps strengthen

the heart-mind connection. Through this balance, we nurture growth across the four sacred dimensions:

Mental: Awareness, clarity, and understanding.

Emotional: Resilience, empathy, and courage to feel deeply.

Spiritual: Connection, guidance, and alignment with purpose.

Physical: Strength, vitality, and harmony with movement.

When these quadrants are in balance, we see how Spiritual and Emotional growth allow us to understand and appreciate life differently. They teach us to embrace change, to honor our emotions, and to seek guidance from Spirit.

How we use our mind and body is determined by our intention and guided by our spiritual and emotional intelligence. Physical and Mental growth come from practicing self-care, overcoming barriers, and realizing our own potential.

We learn that we cannot be broken. Our wholeness remains. Waiting to be remembered. Waiting to be reclaimed.

Learning the Language of the Plants

When these quadrants are in balance, we're ready to receive deeper teachings. **Our ancestral language is inseparable from the land.**

Language and land are one. Evolved over millennia of close observation and shared stories, it encodes the names, characteristics, and interconnections of all beings. To speak our language is to invoke our reciprocal responsibilities: to each other and to the living earth.

Eco-immersion, the practice of deep attunement to the natural world, is how we begin to reawaken this language. By spending extended time on the land, moving at its pace, and engaging all our senses, we gradually attune to the subtle communications flowing between all beings.

We learn to recognize the signs of a plant preparing to flower, the signals of a tree in need of care, the songs of different seasons. We notice how certain plants grow together, which animals rely on their fruits, how they respond to weather patterns. This isn't just observation. **It's conversation.**

As we immerse ourselves, we cultivate an embodied, intuitive understanding that transcends mental concepts. The plants become our teachers, revealing their medicine not just through physical properties, but through the spiritual qualities they embody and awaken within us: Stillness. Resilience. Generosity. Transformation.

We practice. We meditate. We journal our prayers. We remember the scents and sensations of a day spent on the land.

We learn to be present, to listen in the stillness, to share space with spirit.

We often measure ourselves by accomplishments and milestones, as if crossing some invisible finish line proves we've made it. But when we chase these markers, are we living our own vision, or someone else's?

The plants teach us differently.

A plant is vision: Seed. Root. Seedling. Bloom. Show up fully. Gift the world. Transform.

The plants teach us to be present enough to know the vision for ourselves and our families. Not someone else's vision. Not society's finish lines. **Our own.**

They don't need more time. They don't need more things. They need presence.

Our families need presence. Our spirit is presence.

This is love language: gifting our presence. When we understand our purpose, when we live our vision, we find wealth that money cannot buy. **We reconnect to ourselves and to our families who need us. Whole.**

When we manifest our best hopes, when we plan to vibrate long after we're gone, we learn what it means to remain present even when our love transforms. **Love transcends. Language transcends. Presence remains.**

The language we're learning isn't bound to words or sounds. It's the language we were born with: the language of presence, of connection. When we are ready to return, when we are on our path home, **heart is home, spirit is home, whole is home.**

When we live our vision, when we gift our presence to our families and the land, we create something that continues. **We become the teaching. We become the medicine that others will gather long after our earth walk ends.**

In this way, learning the language of the plants is about far more than identification or taxonomy. It is about remembering our rootedness in the web of life. It's about reawakening the wordless yet potent communication that flows between all creatures: the songs of kinship and reciprocity.

Presence is the practice. Presence is the gift. Presence is how we live on.

The Language of Presence

This language reveals itself in the body. Hair standing on end. Overwhelming joy and giddiness that arrives without warning. Wordless knowing rising from the gut.

The plants are our friendliest teachers. They embody everyone who ever showed us true and unconditional love.

Our children remind us of this. They know that gone is just transformation. That our loved ones are the songs in the mountains, the butterflies that come to visit. They can hear us when we say I love you.

This is spirit talking to spirit. We feel it before we think it. We know it before we name it. **We're exactly where we need to be.**

As we nurture our connection, we begin to recognize the many forms of this conversation: felt, seen, intuited. **This is how presence speaks. This is how we continue.**

When We Feel Separated

Barriers are always temporary. They're only as strong as we let them be.

It's alright to feel lost. To feel depressed, anxious, angry. These feelings deserve permission to exist.

When we're angry, we've been hurt. What hurt us? How? What was our part in it? Were we reacting instead of listening?

When we're depressed, we might be thinking about the past without learning from it.

When we're anxious, we might not know where life is taking us, what we want from it.

When we feel lost, when our heart and mind disconnect, these basic needs might be calling: rest, nourishment, connection.

These are not failures. They're invitations.

Make space for what's arising. Journal. Feel it. Name it. Ask: What is this teaching me?

Anger shows us where we need boundaries. Depression shows us where we need to learn from the past, not relive it. Anxiety shows us where we need vision. Loneliness shows us where we need to reconnect heart and mind.

When we give these feelings permission, when we recognize their strength as teaching, they hold less power over us. We learn self-love. We learn to validate ourselves. We learn to give ourselves the same care we give to others.

Then we can let them move through. Not fight them. Not keep them.

Recognize them, learn from them, release them.

We sometimes lose sight of our map, but the path remains. A quick prayer. A deep breath. Remembering the road our heart already knows. **Our heart and spirit have already been where we're going.**

Through patience and openness, what once felt like separation becomes communion.

This is how we learn again to walk in conversation with creation.

We've walked through the foundations of presence, vision, and healing. We've learned that barriers are temporary, that our hearts already know the way home, that the plants embody everyone who ever loved us.

These teachings continue through the seasons.

Spring teaches trust and renewal. Summer teaches discernment and relationship. Fall teaches permission and release. Winter teaches rest and transformation.

Each season carries its own medicine, its own invitation. The plants appear throughout as teachers, as medicine, as the living threads connecting us to ancestors, to land, to each other, and to ourselves.

When you read the stories and teachings ahead, you're learning how knowledge moves: through hands, through loss, through laughter, through generations who still listen.

This is the long handshake. This is how we remember. This is how we continue.

Our Stories

The crackle of fire. The scent of sage smoke. The low murmur of voices carried by the wind. This is how story begins: not as words, but as breath. As the vibration of memory passed between generations.

Stories are how we vibrate after we're gone.

When we tell our stories, we gift our presence to those who will follow. We connect the dots between where we came from, where we are, and where we're going. **Stories give us permission to move beyond what is, to imagine what could be, to strive for more.**

They can be medicine. They can be art. They can be entertainment, escape, humor, grief. They can be the truth, or they can be the truth we're reaching for. **What matters is that we tell them.**

A gifted listener becomes an even greater storyteller. To listen is to hold silence as ceremony, to let the story work within the heart before we give it voice again. This is how wisdom moves from sound to spirit.

Throughout this manuscript, you will find our stories: stand-alone narratives drawn from lived experience, family memory, and the defining moments that have shaped how we learn, teach, and remember.

Some tell our own life stories, our shared walk upon this land. Others honor the lives of those who taught and guided us.

The first of these follows this introduction. As the seasons turn through these pages, each chapter will be graced by its own story, intimately tied to the plants and teachings of that time.

These narratives are not conclusions or morals. They are invitations.

Invitations to pause. To reflect. To connect your own dots. To remember that the deepest knowledge lives not in abstraction, but in the space where memory, relationship, and land entwine.

You have stories too. Stories that carry your presence. Stories that connect your past to your future. Stories that move you beyond what is, toward what you're reaching for.

This is where we listen. This is where we share. This is where we remember.

This story came through dream in early 2020, as the pandemic began.

An ancestor appeared, asking if we knew the plant growing from a crack in the mountain. White Bark Pine. "Yes, yes," excited recognition.

Our heart knew. Knew the plant. Knew the ancestor who could make everything right just by saying: **"I'll take care of it."**

The plant shown in that dream became the medicine we needed. We listened. We trusted our intuition. We connected to ancestral voices telling us what to gather, how to prepare it, when to use it.

When our elders got sick, Grandma helped us make the medicine. She showed us how to bring the ancestors into the making, how love moves through our hands. The medicine worked.

This dream, this medicine, Grandma's teaching—these are the things that make our hearts full when we wonder if we're on the right path.

This is how ancestors take care of it. They teach us to listen, to trust what we know, to follow the guidance that comes through dreams and intuition. Plants become medicine exactly when we need them because we remember how to hear.

Ka papa

Before the humans spoke, the earth spoke first, and I will tell you the story the way my grandfather told me, through the language of the plants, through the magic of our ancestors and for the love of our people.

"High in the mountains where our nupika and ancestors still speak to us, live plants, insects, and animals that are rarely seen. These plants, insects and animals have their own stories and speak their own language (ʔa·kɬukaqwum). This is the story of the plant's gift".

The old chief sang with the wind and strolled along the mountain tops. He gave thanks for the breeze and for the warmth of the morning sun. He offered a song and a prayer to the ancestors before he rested atop a stone. With his weathered hands he felt the stone, his fingers traced each line and crack that told its story. The old chief knew the mountains came to rest here long before his time and they would continue to rest here long after he was gone. In this moment of quiet the chief had a vision and a calm enveloped him. Through this calm the ancestors and nupikaniṅtik invited him to their fires.

Time had passed and the chief could hear children laughing and playing. The sound warmed his heart and called him back from the ancestors and nupikas.
"Nasuʔkin, Papa, kaʔkin kskikiɬ ʔa·qaqna" (*what are you doing?*)
I was up here giving thanks to our ancestors and giving thanks for the children who will carry on our teachings. I was listening to the stories that come from our connection to all things here and now and the beings that are yet to come.
What beings are yet to come? asked one of the children.
The nasuʔkin laughed and said, "after we have something to eat and finish our chores, I will tell you".

Back at camp the children hurried to do their chores, they helped to make food, build fires, and collect water. The chief watched them and noticed they were working hard and moving fast; some of the children even finished their meals before the elders who were served first. While he watched the children's activities he was reminded of the messages from his vision, important lessons he was to pass on. He continued to watch, whilst drinking and eating slowly. The children now watched the nasuʔkin eat and drink, impatiently waiting for him to be done. The chief felt that all eyes were on him in this moment and savored the last bites and drinks from his meal. Next as he always did, he placed his bowl and cup inside each other and folded them in his buckskin. He placed his left hand over the top and gave thanks to creator, the ancestors and to the cooks. Then as always, he would grab his tobacco pouch, take a pinch, and raise it in all directions, he would fill his pipe, inhale, and say, "it is good". Now the children rushed to be by the chief, by the grandfather watching the way he smoked, how he inhaled and nodded his head, how he hmmmmed, just before he was about to say something. The children admiringly gazed upon the nasuʔkin, waiting, and waiting, and waiting for the words that he would speak. The chief cleared his throat, took another puff and hmmmmed again. The children moved anxiously - mouths open waiting for the story. Finally, one of the children chimed in before the chief took another puff . "What beings are coming, you said you would tell us".

"Hmmmm", the chief started. "Ahem", clearing his throat. The ancestors and the nupika told me of our future and our life with some new beings. Do you remember, the rock beings that make up these mountains? Well they have come to rest before our time, and they will rest after our time. The ancestors and the nupika brought me to their fires and told me how to prepare for some newcomers.

Nasu?kin, you have led your kind well. We have observed your patience, your love, and your connection to all things.
It is your love, gratitude and connection that make you a great leader.
It is also your love, gratitude and connection that will make this the hardest lesson you learn.
Each of us has a gift and a purpose, when the newcomers arrive, they will have a purpose and gift, there will be many great leaders amongst them.
Each free moving being of your kind will not move as freely. Your gifts and the way you have lived will soon enter rest like the rock.
The newcomers. They will come in numbers. They will almost outnumber your kind. They will be people.
These people will be grateful, and they will be connected. They will care for their kind. They will be black, white, red, and yellow. They will be on all corners of the earth.
When they come, they will be able to speak the language of the plants, animals, and Creator. They will give thanks and they will be patient, loving, and grateful leaders.
Then when the earth gets smaller, they will be less connected. They will move too fast, and they will be impatient. When they arrive, they will wake up with the knowledge of their connection to all things. Every being will serve them and have a purpose. The people will be grateful, they will give offerings and they will pass on their knowledge.
Plants, animals, and land will gift them with all they need. The people will be reminded that they must always give back.
You, White Bark Pine, are a chief, you will be medicine, you will be shelter, you will be food, you will be a teacher. Today, your kind thrives and exist in numbers. You have cared well for your younglings, elders, and those yet to breathe life.
You and your kind will share a similar path with the red people. Creator has gifted you with beautiful things and the way you will give life. Your purpose will be forgotten by the people and your kind will struggle. People will need trees for shelter among other things. They will forget your purpose and you will watch your kind be decimated, people will create ways that will destroy your roots, they will set fire to the rocks, and they will almost remove your kind from existence.
Those yet to breathe life will have almost no elders, no shelter, and will struggle to have strong roots. The teachings you pass on to your kind will vibrate long after you join the ancestors.
The red people, they will be gifted, and they will manage to connect to their lands. They will take what they need, and they will leave the rest. Then as the world gets smaller, they will welcome newcomers to their land. At first, they will share teachings and remember the

language of the plants. They will have misunderstandings, but they will learn to co-exist and adapt. But like yourself, their purpose will be forgotten.

They will watch the newcomers come in numbers and they will struggle, they will watch their kind be decimated, they will watch them create ways to destroy their roots, they will be removed from their homes, and they will almost be removed from existence.

Those red people yet to breathe life, will have almost no elders, no shelter and will also struggle to have strong roots.

It is your similar paths that will help you to understand each other, it is the similar path that will allow each other's ancestors to communicate, and it is the similar path that will be the strength of your greatest gift.

It is because you have almost lost life, existence, and purpose, that you will be patient enough to gift, life, existence, and purpose.

Your purpose when you leave here will be to teach this to the younglings, to honor your ancestors and to vibrate long after you are gone.

Part Four: Spring
Walking Through Spring

"The land speaks first, teaching us when and how to gather. Our ancestors listened, and now we carry their knowledge forward."

Our ancestors recognized **spring** not just as a time of year, but as a sacred period of awakening. Each plant that emerges tells a story of renewal, carrying teachings passed down through generations.

Before we begin our journey through this season, take a moment to consider your own relationship with renewal.

What changes do you notice in the land around you?
What memories surface when you smell the first thaw, hear the first birds returning, or see the first green pushing through snow?

This connection to seasonal change is part of our traditional understanding. It lives in the body, in the senses, and in the heart's recognition of home.

Spring Equinox: A Time of Balance and Renewal

The **Spring Equinox**, when day and night stand equal, holds profound teachings for our relationship with the plants and the land. This moment of balance reflects the core principles that guide our gathering practices:

Balance in Harvesting: Just as the equinox balances light and darkness, we seek balance in our gathering, *taking only what we need* while ensuring plant communities continue to thrive for the next seven generations.

Renewal and Reciprocity: Spring's emergence mirrors our own renewal of commitments to the land. When we gather plants, we also *give back* through offerings, care, and tending the places where they grow. This is ʔa·knumuɫtiɫiɫ (*Natural Law*), the understanding that everything moves in relationship.

Awakening Awareness: As plants awaken from winter dormancy, *we too awaken our senses* to the subtle changes around us: the first shoots, sap beginning to flow, roots gathering strength before flowering. *To walk in spring is to witness the season of new growth.*

Planting Intentions: Traditionally, seeds planted during this balanced time carry stronger medicine. Likewise, our intentions when approaching plant communities shape the relationships we build. We come not as extractors, but as *relatives returning to tend and learn.*

The Equinox reminds us that our relationships with plants exist within larger natural cycles.
By aligning our practices with these cycles, we honor both the

plants and the ancestral knowledge that continues to guide us.

First Steps: Introducing Ourselves to the Land

Before we gather a single plant, we practice one of our most essential protocols: introducing ourselves to the land.

When we enter a gathering place, we begin by speaking our names, given or traditional, to the land and all beings present.

We acknowledge that we have returned to continue our learning journey and to carry forward the teachings of those who came before us.

This introduction isn't merely a formality. It is a recognition of relationship and respect. An acknowledgment that we are guests, even on the lands of our ancestors.

A Simple Introduction:

"My name is _____.

I come to learn and gather with respect. I acknowledge the ancestors who walked here before me and carry their wisdom forward. I offer tobacco [or sage, or a strand of my hair, or a song] as thanks for what I am about to receive."

Through this simple act, we remind ourselves that we are never alone on the land. We are always in the company of ancestors, future generations, and all living beings who share this space with us.

Some of us also ask the plants directly:

"Do you have medicine to share today?

Which of you is ready to teach me?"

Then we listen. With our bodies, our intuition, our quiet attention. For the answer. Once we have properly introduced ourselves and received permission, we can begin to observe and learn from the plants that are ready to share their gifts.

The Medicine of Gratitude

Gratitude is the oldest medicine. It is the first prayer when we wake, the last before we rest, and the quiet heartbeat carrying us through everything in between.

When we move through life with gratitude, the world opens. The plants respond differently. The wind feels softer. Challenges carry teachings.

Gratitude does not erase pain or struggle. It transforms them.
It helps us see that even in difficulty, something sacred is still growing.

The land has shown us that gratitude is a living exchange.

In our way, gratitude is never silent. It moves through action: through offering, sharing, tending. To live with gratitude is to live in ceremony.

Our children remind us of this. They thank the world without hesitation. They know gratitude is not something we practice. It is something we are born with.

Every time we gather plants, light a smudge, or prepare food for the people, we feel our ancestors close. We hear their voices:

Always give thanks before you take.
Always give thanks before you speak.
Always give thanks before you rise.

Gratitude humbles us. It reminds us that we are part of something vast. Our breath belongs to the same rhythm as the trees, the waters, and the stars.

It teaches us to walk gently, to live with intention, and to love without measure.

When we speak gratitude, we feel it move through our bodies.

It reminds us that no matter how far we wander, we are always carried by the kindness of creation.

Gratitude is the medicine that heals the space between us. It is the bridge between the seen and unseen, the root of all connection, the song that never ends.

Trust and the Unknown

When we let go of the rush, when we stop trying to prove that our knowledge belongs, the land begins to show us that it already does. Our work is recognized not through striving, but through right timing, through trust, and through living what we know.

Spring is the season of trust. Seeds trust the soil will feed them. Roots trust the earth will hold them. Plants trust the sun will return. **We trust that what has slept through winter will awaken in its own time.**

Trust does not ask for certainty. It is a relationship with the unseen. A quiet agreement between heart and earth. It asks us to keep showing up, to keep listening, even when the path ahead is hidden.

When we introduce ourselves to the land, we trust that relationship is real, even if unseen. When we teach our children the languages of our ancestors, we trust those words will find their way home. **When we grieve, we trust that love continues in another form.**

Trust is the medicine that guides us through the unknown: the space between endings and beginnings, where transformation waits.

Reflection: The Teachings of Spring

Spring teaches us to trust renewal.

Even when we have forgotten ourselves, the earth remembers.

The plants remind us that new beginnings do not ask for perfection. They ask for presence. To show up. To open. To begin again.

The thaw is slow, but sure. The roots do not rush, and yet everything changes.

Each step we take into spring is a small act of faith: a promise to participate in life's unfolding.

We have walked through meaningful losses. Each one a teacher. These moments, though painful, became part of the medicine of understanding. They reminded us that healing and grief move side by side, that love and absence are not opposites, but continuations of one another.

The spirits of those who walked before us still move within these pages. Their laughter, their teachings, their quiet prayers carried in every season. They remind us that love never truly leaves. It transforms.

"Why didn't you tell me you were coming?"

A question that lingers somewhere between worlds, both tender and eternal. And after all these years, through our own growth, we have found the answer:

Because we wanted to be present. Because presence is how love endures.

Spring reminds us that love never ends. It simply changes form. Every thaw, every loss, every new leaf is another way the world says:

Begin again.

Spring Equinox Prayer

Creator, we thank You for the return of light, for the way water moves again, for the sound of melt, for the scent of earth rising.

We ask to awaken gently, to open like the willow buds, to stretch like the roots of dandelion seeking sun.

May what has rested beneath snow return strong and sure. May we remember that even the smallest sprout carries great promise.

For all that was, we give thanks. For all that is returning, we give thanks. For all that will bloom, we give thanks.

—Prayer of Renewal, Keepers of the Seasons

Spring has taught us to trust renewal. To stop proving we belong and simply show up. To remember that presence, not perfection, is how love endures.

We have learned to begin again.

As we move into summer, these teachings deepen. We will learn what to tend, what to nourish, what deserves our discernment. We will practice relationship with the abundance the land offers.

First, the plants themselves. Each one a teacher. Each one carrying the medicine of renewal, reciprocity, and return.

Kanuhus ʔa·knuq̓yuk̓ naʔuti

Kanuhus ʔa·knuq̓yuk̓ naʔuti was picking plants and singing in the garden. She was singing while saying good morning to all the little critters in the yard and sky.

"Good morning butterfly, you fly so pretty, Good morning grasshopper you jump so high. Good morning sun, you shine so bright and warm".

"Kaʼs kiʔin, granddaughter," called out titi qʼu¢ac. It's time to go out to pick naqam¢u today, my girl. Today, titi would teach Kanuhus ʔa·knuq̓yuk̓ naʔuti about the naqam¢u. Titi used it for food like soups, or sweet for dessert, or dry for winter. She would also share it with her friends. "Where are we going?" asked, Red Flower Girl. "We are going over the bluff and out to the prairie, my girl. I will teach you the ways to gather our precious plant". So off went titi and Red Flower Girl. They talked and sang the whole way to the prairie. Red Flower Girl sang and skipped the whole way. Titi smiled at her beautiful granddaughter. Titi and Red Flower Girl had been walking for a long time. Titi stopped and sat on a rock and started to sing. She sang so beautiful thought Red Flower Girl. Titi sang an old song that her titi taught her. Titi gave thanks for the day, to the water, and sun that gave nourishment to the bitterroot. She gave thanks to creator and mother earth. While titi sang, Red Flower Girl danced and danced, she twirled and twirled. "Red Flower Girl, it's your turn to sing", said titi. Red Flower Girl sang and sang and sang. She twirled and twirled until she couldn't stand any longer. She was laughing and giggling and laying in the field. When Red Flower Girl opened her eyes, she was surrounded by green spiders. "Titi"! cried Red Flower Girl. "There are so many spiders around me help!"

Titi sat on her rock laughing. "Oh, my girl, those aren't spiders. That's the bitterroot and that's the plant we came to pick."

"Oh, this is why we came out here and this is the plant that you make berry soup from and that you dry for winter and that you share with our aunties. How come they look like that, with flowers and some look like spiders"?

"Well, granddaughter, some look like spiders and some have flowers because that's how Creator made them. They all have purpose and are at different stages of development, but they are all special".

"You mean like how you, grasshopper, butterfly, and my brothers and sisters all have different looks"?

"Yes, Granddaughter, and that's what makes everything on Creator's earth precious and special. We all have a purpose and a gift. Today your new gift is the song I taught you and the plant I showed you". Titi and Red Flower Girl picked bitterroot for the rest of the day.

They sang the song over and over. They picked, and they picked, and they laughed and told stories. Later, when they had finally gathered enough bitterroot they went home. On the way home, Red Flower Girl saw a frog by the creek and a fawn playing with her mother. She was grateful for all the beauty she saw today. Red Flower Girl looked at her titi and thought of the great adventure they had today and thought this is the best day ever!

When they finally got home, Red Flower Girl ran off to go play and tell her brothers and sisters all about her day. She talked about granny and the frog, the baby deer and all the bitterroot they gathered.

The end.

ʔa·kuwaɫwuʔk, Birch Tree/Paper Birch *(Betula papyrifera)*

(Edible / Medicinal / Spiritual / Practical)

Traditional Uses and Personal Experience

Many of us have early memories of birch bark: peeling the papery layers, learning to make *naʔhik* (picking baskets), being taught ancestral skills our grandparents carried. We have been blessed with mentors for whom this way of life was only like yesterday. The more we work with these practices, the more ancestral muscle memory awakens. The skills come naturally, as if our hands remember what our minds are just learning.

Birch has always been a plant of many gifts. The bark served as fire-starter, material for baskets and canoes, and cookware. It also provided nutrition: chewed fresh, stripped into noodles, or ground into flour as emergency food during difficult times.

Our ancestors' ingenuity shows in how they used birch bark for cooking. Containers were waterproofed with sap and charcoal mixed into sealing glue, or lined with hide and heated with hot rocks to boil water.

Towards the end of winter, we collect birch water: a pleasant-tasting drink much like coconut water mixed with earthy fresh spring water. It can be drunk straight from the tree. The tapping season is short (4 weeks) and best done early in spring. Once harvested, use the water within 2-7 days. We take care not to over-harvest, ensuring the tree's continued health.

The birch water collected in spring was used for cleansing after long winter months. When people became deficient in vitamins and nutrients during winter, the birch water, along with the cambium layer, offered essential replenishment and early treatment.

Health Benefits

Water is rich in **manganese, magnesium, calcium, zinc, and copper** and low in natural sugars. Birch water offers numerous *minerals and antioxidants* and improves **skin and hair health**.

Habitat and Description

Along creeks, rivers, and streams growing in colonies through their rhizomatous nature. Deciduous tree, **10–30 m tall,** distinctive **white to reddish brown bark**. Prefer moist to mesic woodlands, forests, clearcuts, and open areas (lowland, steppe, montane).

kanuɬmaquɬaqpiʔk, Cottonwood
(Populus balsamifera)

(Edible / Medicinal / Spiritual / Practical)

Traditional Uses and Cultural Significance

Cottonwood has been valued for generations, especially for smoking meat: a process that infuses food with both flavor and preservation.

As one of the earliest spring plants to offer medicine, we eagerly await its late spring blooms. The unmistakable sweet, resinous fragrance makes this plant easy to identify.

After a day gathering cottonwood buds, our hands are dark and tarry with resin. This is the work: ensuring we have enough to share, enough for the oils and salves we make. Cottonwood lends its scent and flavor to everything it touches.

Cottonwood buds were one of the first plants we visited after losing Grumpa. They reminded us of how we live our lives and how we are present after we are gone.

Health Benefits

Beyond our traditional use for smoking meats, cottonwood offers significant medicinal value. The **inner bark or cambium layer** provides a natural source of **vitamin C**, particularly valuable during early spring when fresh foods were historically scarce.

Great for **skin care when infused in oil**, cottonwood has **pain-relieving attributes** and can enhance the effects of salves and balms when used with other plants.

Habitat and Description

A **deciduous, dioecious (male and female) tree** that can grow to **50 meters tall** with **triangular, egg-shaped or heart-shaped leaves**. The leaves are **finely toothed** and **white to pale green on the underside**. The tree expresses itself through **male and female catkins; male catkins measuring 2-3 cm long** with distinctive **yellow coloration**, while **female catkins extend 8-20 cm**.

Found in **moist uplands and floodplains (montane)**.

waʔta, Spring Beauty *(Claytonia lanceolata)*

(Edible / Medicinal / Spiritual)

Traditional Uses and Cultural Significance

The early days of taking our daughter on the land have been precious. One of the times she most enjoyed salad was when we made her a mix of spring greens: Spring Beauty flowers, Glacier lily flowers and leaves, with a few boiled pieces of spring beauty bulb. Watching her enjoy our first ancestral foods was a privilege and gift.

First foods, early medicines, and new learners remind us why this knowledge matters. The quick season makes waiting and finding them exciting. Once you've seen one plant in flower, they all seem to appear at once. In a few days there can be abundance, or just as fast as they arrived, they are gone.

Most of the plant is edible and used in many ways. The corm (bulb) can be cooked similar to camas, then dehydrated and ground into flour. This flour was used to thicken broths, make breads, or add to pemmican.

Ktunaxa and Interior Salish traditionally use both bulbs and greens. The leaves make a good first foods salad (use sparingly), while bulbs are typically pit-cooked as a side dish. The bulbs can be prepared like potatoes with contemporary ingredients, adding a water-chestnut-like crunch to soups and stews.

Health Benefits

This plant is what we would refer to as a **complex carbohydrate**, as the plant takes longer to digest and doesn't spike glucose/insulin levels, making it a **diabetes-friendly food**. High in **vitamins A and C. High in nutritional value.**

Habitat and Description

Easily identified by its **white to light pink flower with a fine pink stripe down the petals**. Each flower is about **1/3 inch across**, consists of **2 green sepals** with **5 stamens with pink anthers**.

Perennial that grows from a **spherical underground corm** bearing fibrous roots. Found in **moist, nutrient-rich soils of the forest**, favoring the **forest edges that receive a good amount of sunlight**. Found in **moist meadows, shrublands, grasslands, and snow bed sites (steppe, alpine zones)**.

ȼuʔkuna, Stinging Nettle *(Urtica dioica)*

(Edible / Medicinal / Spiritual / Practical)

Traditional Uses and Cultural Significance

Stinging nettles are one of the most respected and versatile plants in both traditional and contemporary medicine. They emerge early in spring, offering medicine to cleanse and strengthen the body after winter.

Nettles entered our lives when pharmaceuticals stopped working for tension headaches. The plant offered relief, working with the body rather than against it. We learned to harvest nettle with care, understanding how to handle its sting without fear. This was one of the first plants we deeply connected with.

Among Indigenous communities, nettles have been used for centuries. Young plants can be cooked to neutralize their sting and eaten like spinach, while fibrous stalks can be processed into thread for nets and textiles. Urtication (rubbing fresh nettles on sore joints) stimulates circulation and reduces inflammation.

Health Benefits

Stinging nettles are powerful spring medicine used for **detoxifying**. They provide **blood and liver support**, cleansing toxins and supporting kidney and liver function. The plant offers **pain relief**, alleviating arthritis, muscle tension, and joint pain. Nettles act as a natural **antihistamine** for allergy support, while also supporting **reproductive health**, including fertility and menstrual regulation.

Habitat and Description

Perennial herb growing **1-2 meters tall** with **oval leaves and serrated edges**. Covered in distinctive **stinging hairs that release formic acid** when touched.

Thrives in **moist, rich soils along rivers, meadows, and disturbed ground**. Found throughout BC and Montana in **streamsides, woodlands, and floodplains**.

ʔa·ʼq̓uku kaɬmuxu, Woodland Strawberry *(Fragaria virginiana)*

(Edible / Medicinal / Spiritual / Practical)

Traditional Uses and Cultural Significance

Wild strawberries are a cherished treat that ripen from late spring into early summer. Since our daughter's first taste, this has quickly become a favorite. As soon as the snow clears, she impatiently checks on the strawberry plants. This plant is also a favored food source for woodland animals and insects, reminding us that the early bird gets the worm.

This is one of the plants connected to the cough medicine we made with tŭpyeʔ (Grandma). The memories held here carry forward: songs, laughter, the beauty of those we love.

Nearly every part of the plant can be used. From eating the fresh fruit to making tea with the leaves and runners. The fruits can be enjoyed fresh or preserved in jams and jellies. In our family, we regularly use the leaves and runners in tea blends and cold medicine mixes, finding they add both flavor and healing properties.

First Nations traditionally powdered leaves for treating sores, informing our practices today.

Health Benefits

Rich in **vitamin C**, wild strawberries support overall health. Traditionally, the plant has been used to **regulate the menstrual cycle and support milk production**, reflecting its role in women's health and nourishment.

Habitat and Description

Low-growing perennial with **fibrous roots** and **egg-shaped basal leaves with fine serrations**. Blooms with **delicate white flowers with five petals**, each **1–2 cm wide** with a **bright yellow center** formed by the stamens. Spreads through **"runners"**.

Thrives in **wooded, gravelly areas with moderate to full sun**. Found in **moist to dry fields, meadows, and open forests** across **lowland and subalpine zones**.

qaɬukp, Yellowbells *(Fritillaria pudica)*

(Edible / Medicinal / Spiritual)

Traditional Uses and Cultural Significance
Yellowbell is another of the early foods in our ancestral diet: small in status but high in nutritional content. This plant can first be observed after the snow melts.

To some, this food fresh out of the ground has an acquired taste and mouth feel, similar to eating a ball of lard or shortening. Spiritually, it links us to our ancestors and brings insight into the traditional diet and food as medicine. Much like the harvesting of animals, we appreciate a portion of the bounty straight from the earth.

This plant has been used similarly to spring beauty: boiled, dried, and preserved for later consumption.

Over the years, yellowbell has appeared scarce in places we once found it abundant. Traveling, seasonal timing, logging practices, all shift where and when we encounter them. **As we've practiced more intentional stewardship, giving places rest, some populations have returned stronger.**

This plant teaches us about relationship with the natural world. **How do we meet this plant where it is, rather than where we expect it to be?**

Health Benefits
As with most starchy foods, this plant offers **carbohydrates and fiber**. It doesn't spike glucose/insulin levels, making it **diabetes-friendly and heart healthy**.

Habitat and Description
Perennial herb grows from a **bulb** with **lanceolate leaves 3-15 cm long**. The plant with flower can stand **4 to 10 inches tall** with a **yellow, bell-shaped, nodding flower**. The sepals and petals share similar color.Found in **high plains, grasslands, and drier ponderosa forests** at **low to mid elevations**. Prefers **full sun with good drainage** in **gravelly to rocky soil.good drainage** in **gravelly to rocky soil.**

ʔinq̓um, Skunk Cabbage *(Lysichiton americanus)*

(Edible / Medicinal / Spiritual / Practical)

Traditional Uses and Cultural Significance

Skunk cabbage is primarily valued for its cultural and practical uses rather than as a food source. Its large, durable leaves have long been used in pit-cooking to insulate food from dirt, hot rocks, and embers. We observed this practice as children at culture camps, and we continue to use the leaves during personal gatherings, especially to protect our camas bulbs during cooking.

As adults, this was another plant where we got to harvest alongside our elders. Not only showing or telling us where to go or what to look for, they waded through the water, pushed through the grass, and helped us harvest and pack to our vehicle.

The plant's broad leaves are also well-suited as berry-drying mats, and they serve practical roles as cups, plates, and containers for harvesting or serving food.

Medicinally, the roots have been burned and inhaled as smoke treatment for coughs and respiratory ailments, while warm leaves have been applied as compresses for rheumatism.

Although some elders have experimented with eating the young leaves, most find the taste unpleasant. The roots and young shoots can be consumed with proper preparation.

Health Benefits

The roots provide smoke treatment for coughs and respiratory ailments when burned and inhaled. Warm leaves serve as compresses for rheumatism.

Habitat and Description

Semi-aquatic perennial herb grows from a thick rhizome with fibrous roots. Its large, egg-shaped to lanceolate leaves emerge from the base and can reach impressive sizes. In early spring, skunk cabbage produces a **yellow hood-like spathe** that surrounds a spike of small green-yellow flowers. These flowers emit a distinctive odor that attracts pollinators and gives the plant its name. Prefers moist, shaded environments, thriving in wetlands, swamps, forested seeps, and along ditches in both lowland and montane zones.

Red Clover *(Trifolium pratense)*

(Edible / Medicinal / Spiritual / Practical)

Traditional Uses and Cultural Significance

Spotted from a mile away, this gentle plant offers a calming and comforting experience. The soft pink to red flower heads are inviting to small children and pollinators. We gather this plant anytime from May through October, using most parts of the plant. The teas are mild, soothing, and comforting with pleasant floral undertones.

Red Clover is a staple in women's wellness tea blends. It supports the body through hormonal transitions: menstrual cycles, fertility, menopause. **The ritual of making the tea, boiling water, steeping, sitting with warmth, is part of the healing.**

We work with families reconnecting to ceremony, to land-based practice, to ways of being that got interrupted. Red Clover tea becomes part of that reconnection: the ritual of slowing down, of warmth, of listening to what the body needs.

For some children, this practice helps them honor their sensitivity rather than learning to suppress it.

Health Benefits

Red Clover contains **isoflavones** that gently interact with estrogen receptors, supporting hormonal rhythm rather than disrupting it. The plant provides calcium, magnesium, niacin, potassium, and vitamin C. Benefits include support for heart health, nervous system calming, and general cleansing. Its medicine helps relieve symptoms of stress, anxiety, and spiritual overwhelm.

Habitat and Description

Perennial herb grows from a taproot with soft, hairy stems usually **20-70 cm tall**. Leaves are **trifoliate (three-part)**, forming sacred triads. Each round **pink-purple flower head** contains **50-200 tiny florets**.

Found in **fields, meadows, and roadsides** across lowland, steppe, and montane zones.

Oxeye Daisy *(Leucanthemum vulgare)*

(Edible / Medicinal / Spiritual / Practical)

Traditional Uses and Cultural Significance

Though not native to North America, this plant has become part of our local ecology, supporting numerous pollinators through its long flowering period from May to October. We are often reminded of the bees when we see this plant, watching the many visitors that come to these flowers.

Medicine isn't about origin. It's about relationship. Oxeye Daisy has learned how to belong, offering long-blooming floral resources when many native plants have gone to seed.

Children are often drawn to these flowers instinctively, making daisy chains or tucking them behind ears: a reminder of the freedom of play and the wisdom of small things.

The leaves can be eaten raw or cooked, added sparingly to sandwiches, wraps, tacos, or salads. Young spring shoots finely chopped enhance salads. Flowers brewed as tea ease coughs and bronchial issues.

Health Benefits

The whole plant, especially the flowers, has medicinal properties that are **antispasmodic, cough-relieving, diuretic, and wound-healing**. Rich in **vitamin C and polyphenols**, oxeye daisy offers antioxidant benefits. It has been used in the treatment of whooping cough, asthma, and nervous excitability, acting similarly to chamomile as a calming tonic. Externally, flowers can be used as **gentle washes for wounds** or as a **hand rinse for chapped hands**, especially meaningful for those who work with the land. A cooled tea can serve as a gentle skin rinse for irritated or tired hands.

Habitat and Description

Perennial grows **20-80 cm tall** with alternating **spoon-shaped leaves** that are hairless or soft-hairy. Basal leaves are broad with narrow lobes to blunt teeth. The **white ray flowers** surround a **yellow disc center**, with bracts that have a narrow, dark-brown band. Thrives in **disturbed soils**, including roadsides, pastures, waste areas, and grasslands at low to mid-elevations.

Mountain Lady's Slipper
(Cypripedium montanum)

(Edible / Medicinal / Spiritual / Practical)

Traditional Uses and Cultural Significance

Our Uncle Clark shared how this orchid has traditionally supported memory, clarity, and cognitive function, particularly as we age. The roots were historically dried, powdered, or tinctured to relieve headaches, emotional stress, and menstrual discomfort. This medicine also serves students, those under high stress, and anyone needing to call spirit back to mind.

Uncle Clark shared this knowledge so it would go forward. We share it for the same reason: so that when the medicine is needed, people know what to look for.

But the deeper teaching goes beyond remedy. It's about knowing when not to touch, when presence is the medicine.

Medicine begins long before any plant is touched. To kneel beside it in silence is ceremony.

This plant asks us to consider: **For those whose minds we worry about losing, are we taking time to sit and listen, to have a meal, to walk together? Or are we looking for medicine hoping it fixes what only presence can heal?**

Are we willing to do the work alongside the plant?

Given its slow growth and extreme sensitivity, we often choose to observe rather than harvest. But when the medicine is truly needed, we make that decision carefully, knowing what we're asking for and what we're willing to give in return.

Health Benefits

This orchid offers gentle relief from **anxiety, sleeplessness, and muscle tension** stored from emotional pain. It supports **neurological health**, aiding memory and clarity, especially for age-related cognitive decline. This is **slow medicine**: benefits felt as deep rest, not loud or immediate effects.

Habitat and Description

Brownish-purple sepals frame a **slipper-shaped white lip with deep magenta veins**, blooming **May to June** in **montane forests**. Rarely above **30 cm tall**, but its presence is unmistakable.

Fairy Slipper *(Calypso bulbosa)*

(Edible / Medicinal / Spiritual / Practical)

Traditional Uses and Cultural Significance

We have honored Fairy Slipper's bulbs for their buttery taste and antispasmodic properties. We've used it sparingly. This plant teaches us to approach with care, to do broader research across ancestral teachings, and to remember that all knowledge can live inside us when we carry it with respect.

Fairy Slipper grows in community. Never alone. Always amongst other plants, pollinators, and protectors. Finding sun, water, and nutrition together. When shaded, they show resilience not through isolation. Through connection.

This plant reminds us: What might feel like important work should never supersede the importance of family life and responsibilities. Yes, it may be our responsibility to teach, but who do we teach first? It might be our responsibility to nourish, but who eats first? Who gets our first serving?

We attune ourselves to the Guiding Principles of ʔa·knumu¢titił when approaching this plant. And when approaching our own lives. The work matters. **Home matters first.**

Health Benefits

Traditionally used to **ease tension, calm nerves, and support memory**. The bulbs offer **antispasmodic properties**, particularly helpful for emotional stress and muscle tension stored in the body.

Its real power may lie in **presence rather than prescription.** A plant that reminds us to be present, to feel our space, nurture our heart-mind connection, to have patience, and to remember. We are enough.

Habitat and Description

Small orchid grows **5–22 cm tall**, with a **nodding, pink-purple flower** on a single stem. Its **yellow, hooded lip** gives off a soft **vanilla scent**.

Thrives in **shaded coniferous forests** rich in humus, **always in community with other plants**.

ʔa·knuq̓yuk̓, Violet *(Viola spp)*

(Edible / Medicinal / Spiritual / Practical)

Traditional Uses and Cultural Significance

Violets can be found in a variety of colors (yellow, white, blue, purple) and have similar traits in the way they are used. We have found relief with this plant for debilitating tension headaches after pharmaceutical options were no longer viable. Violet tea mixed with a few other plants, along with medicinal smoke mixes, offered gentle medicine when it was needed.

Medicine is connection. The way we honor our plant allies mirrors the way we honor our relationships. With validation, not dismissal. Violet teaches us that pain is real, experiences are real, and we don't have to just "deal with it." We can acknowledge what's true and still move toward thriving, not just surviving.

On our nature walks, we often eat a few of these flowers alongside wild strawberries. A way of being present with what the land offers. Ayla has taken a liking to eating fresh flowers, learning early that medicine can be gentle, accessible, and part of everyday connection.

We make syrups and jellies from violets. Seasonal treats loved by our respected elders. We also use violets in sparkling tonics, teas, and smoke mixes.

Health Benefits

This plant is high in **Vitamins A and C**. It offers **anti-inflammatory, expectorant, and antirheumatic properties**. Our personal use and experience have been for **headaches, colds, and pain relief** in addition to our usage as food. The gentle nature of violet makes it suitable for regular use without harsh effects.

Habitat and Description

Perennial herb grows from a scaly, fleshy rhizome without stolons (**5-30 cm tall**). Leaves grow basally and appear **heart-shaped to kidney-shaped** with toothed or serrated edges. Single flowers feature **five petals** in various colors including **purple, blue, white, and yellow**, with the lower petal measuring 8-14 mm.

Grows along **mesic to moist streambanks, woodlands, clearings, and forest** at all elevations from **lowland to alpine zones**. This wide distribution makes violets accessible to many communities across different landscapes.

Xapi, Camas *(Camassia quamash)*

(Edible / Medicinal / Spiritual / Practical)

Traditional Uses and Cultural Significance

Camas brings joy to our hearts. We have harvested for many years and grown deep appreciation and gratitude for all this plant offers. We dehydrate the cooked bulbs and use them as a thickening agent in jams and jellies, soups and stews. Honoring preservation practices that live in our blood memory. We've complemented it with other flours to make breads and sweet treats.

Camas reminds us of Grumpa. We were able to capture him harvesting this plant for what would be his first and last time, with Ayla by his side. Our relationship was complicated, but we're glad we stayed open enough to see him as he was before he crossed over. Ayla asks sometimes, "Do you miss Grumpa?" She's not scared to ask, and we're not scared to answer. "We sure do. Do you?"

Camas grows where the plants speak, and we still see him there.

Our camas harvests have become occasions for family gatherings, pit cooks, and feasts. Times of laughter, nourishment, and making new memories rooted in old ways.

Health Benefits

The bulbs contain **inulin**, a prebiotic fiber that supports **gut health and helps regulate blood sugar**. Camas provides essential **carbohydrates and some protein**, making it a valuable food source.

CRITICAL: Death camas is highly poisonous and can look similar to edible camas. **Harvest with a friend or mentor who knows the plant.** Ask questions, observe closely, stay curious and vigilant. **When in doubt, do not harvest.**

Habitat and Description

Perennial plant grows from a bulb with **grass-like leaves**. Produces **star-shaped, blue to deep blue flowers** in late spring to early summer, growing in clusters atop stems that reach **20-80 cm in height**. Thrives in **well-drained soils high in humus**, often in **open meadows, prairies, and along streams and rivers**. Native to western North America, found throughout the northwestern United States and southern Canada.

Note: Traditional management included controlled burning to enhance camas meadows. After a recent wildfire near Arlee, Montana, camas emerged in areas where it hadn't been for many years.

ʔaɫa, Edible Horsehair *(Bryoria fremontii)*

(Edible / Medicinal / Spiritual / Practical)

Traditional Uses and Cultural Significance

We have both heard the coyote stories about how this lichen came to be. Teachings that remind us every plant has its own narrative.

Mix horsehair lichen with ʔiɫwas (tree sap) for chewing gum. Grandparents' knowledge, passed from their grandparents. They taught us in the moment, on the land, the way they learned.

We've also been taught to use horsehair lichen paired with yarrow to pack a wound. Other practical uses include diaper lining and in pit cooking as an insulator, flavoring agent, and flavor retainer. The long, hair-like strands that hang from tree branches have served families for generations. Sustenance, medicine, and practical technology.

Health Benefits

Used in traditional medicine for **digestive issues** and as a **poultice for swellings**. Our people have used it for **baby medicines, bandages, and as a general tonic**. Our teachers shared that it can be used to **remove warts**.

Although its carbohydrates are not digestible by humans, it can **increase the nutritional value of other foods when cooked together**, absorbing starches from other foods during pit cooking.

Habitat and Description

This lichen grows on **coniferous trees**, its **hair-like strands** draping from branches. Found in **dense, old-growth forests**, often high in the canopy where air circulates freely.

Sensitive to pollution and disturbance, its presence signals a healthy, balanced forest system.

Maxa, Glacier Lily *(Erythronium grandiflorum)*

(Edible/Medicinal/Spiritual/Practical)

Traditional Uses and Cultural Significance

Maxa was one of Ayla's first introductions to the land's generosity. She plucks them joyfully, offering each bloom as a gift, tasting the tender parts with curiosity and delight.

We prepare the bulbs and leaves in early spring salads with homemade vinaigrette. Traditionally, the bulbs were boiled, dried, and simmered in stews. Important food when winter stores ran low.

Maxa has led us to deeper thinking. Not just identifying a pretty flower, but observing, connecting, asking what it might offer. This is how we attune when personal experience makes us wonder: what plants can help? How do we mitigate before crisis?

We've observed that maxa thrives after fire. Our ancestors used controlled burns, and we continue to see this relationship: after wildfire, glacier lilies return vigorously.

Health Benefits

The **corms** were traditionally used to support recovery from **colds, reduce fevers, and ease swelling or infection**. Pulverized roots were applied to **boils and skin sores**.

Rich in **natural starches and carbohydrates**, the bulbs offered much-needed energy in early spring. The **leaves and seedpods** also hold nutritional value, making maxa an important spring offering when other foods were still scarce.

Habitat and Description

Produces **bright yellow, nodding flowers** with **six backward-curved tepals**, rising solitary on stalks up to **30 cm tall**. Two **basal leaves, lance-shaped and gently wavy**, emerge from a deep underground bulb.

One of the **first plants to bloom as snow recedes**, signaling spring's arrival. Found from **April through August** depending on elevation, thrives in **moist subalpine meadows, forest openings, and mountain slopes**.

ʼkitʼquꝉkaꝉmaxaka, Dandelion
(Taraxacum officinale)

(Edible / Medicinal / Spiritual / Practical)

Traditional Uses and Cultural Significance

Dandelion, with its golden mane, persists even as frost brushes the land. Offering nourishment when most plants begin their rest. Around our home, it continues to bloom and give well into late fall.

We roast the roots as part of herbal coffee blends, making it a beloved ingredient in many seasonal drinks. Ayla loves blowing away the seeds, watching the puffs fly while the dogs chasing them.

This plant shows up where it's needed. Roadsides, lawns, disturbed spaces. And makes itself useful. We turn to it for liver and kidney support, digestion, and cleansing.

Health Benefits

Offers **diuretic, anti-inflammatory, and antioxidant** support. The **leaves** bring **vitamins A, C, and K**, along with **potassium and iron**. The **roots** help purify and strengthen the body—especially helpful for **digestive stagnation or fatigue**.

Habitat and Description

Grows low to the ground with a **rosette of jagged leaves** and hollow stalks. Its **taproot can reach 15–30 cm deep**. **Bright yellow flowers** open to the light and close in darkness, blooming from **early spring through late fall**.

Found in **temperate climates**, thrives in **moist soils**—especially along roadsides, lawns, and disturbed spaces.

Xaɫ, Arrowleaf Balsamroot
(Balsamorhiza sagittata)

(Edible / Medicinal / Spiritual / Practical)

Traditional Uses and Cultural Significance

Xaɫ is one of the first foods we personally began harvesting in early spring. It has long been a source of nourishment, particularly during lean times when other food sources were scarce. The roots, though fibrous and woody throughout most of the year, can be peeled and processed to provide nutrition.

In our cooking presentations, we've used the roots creatively. Frying them into decorative "nests" as part of Indigenous food displays that celebrate both form and function.

Its high sap content makes it powerful in oil infusions, which we use to treat wounds, muscle aches, and seasonal illness.

The flowers emerge before the plant's large arrow-shaped leaves fully develop, often while snow still clings to north-facing slopes. Announcing spring's arrival.

Health Benefits

Offers **antibacterial, antifungal, and expectorant** properties. The **roots** are particularly helpful for **respiratory issues**, assisting in **loosening and clearing mucus from the lungs**.

Infused into oils, it becomes a soothing base for **salves used on wounds, burns, bruises, and aching muscles**.

Young leaves and shoots are rich in **vitamins A and C, calcium, and antioxidants**. Offering nourishment in early spring when other foods are scarce.

Habitat and Description

Thrives on dry, sunny hillsides, meadows, and south-facing slopes. Brilliant, sunflower-like blossoms with bright yellow ray florets surrounding a central disc create vibrant clusters. The fuzzy, grey-green leaves can grow impressively large.

Its **deep taproot system** allows it to survive in **drought-prone areas**. Among the **earliest to emerge** in spring.

Trillium *(Trillium ovatum)*

(Edible / Medicinal / Spiritual / Practical)

Traditional Uses and Cultural Significance

Western Trillium serves as a seasonal marker. This plant holds deep significance in women's health. Many nations prepared root decoctions to support menstruation and childbirth.

Broad knowledge is the great gift we can give ourselves. Whether formal education, plant classes, or learning from knowledge holders. To use and exercise our brain, the way we move through the world. Our knowledge isn't set to one way of teaching or singular knowledge streams. We teach through hands-on experience, through asking questions, through getting things wrong and still going.

We watch when the animals are more active. When the robins start nesting. When the pollinators are searching for new blossoms. We don't always look for Trillium, respecting its growth cycle. Some plant medicines are requested and we will harvest. Others, we make note of and return to the areas if asked.

We attune ourselves to the Guiding Principles of ʔa·knumuȼtiɬiɬ when approaching this plant, knowing its slow growth makes it vulnerable.

Health Benefits

Trillium root is known for its **antiseptic, diuretic, and uterine-stimulating** properties. Cultural teachings detail its preparation for addressing **respiratory issues, infections of the eyes and ears, and reproductive health**.

In times of survival or emergency, properly prepared **leaves** provided a source of nutrition when other foods were scarce.

Habitat and Description

Produces a single, **three-petaled bloom** that shifts from **white to pink** as it matures, marking its pollination phase. The flower emerges above **three ovate leaves arranged in perfect symmetry**, blooming in **coniferous forests** dominated by spruce and fir.

Thrives in **mesic, humus-rich soils** with reliable drainage and **partial shade**, often at lower to mid-elevations. Its **slow-growing rhizomatous root system** makes it highly susceptible to overharvesting—this is why we only gather in true need.

Naqamȼu, Bitterroot *(Lewisia rediviva)*

(Edible / Medicinal / Spiritual / Practical)

Traditional Uses and Cultural Significance

Our mothers, knowledge holders, and elders passed on the tradition of returning the heart and head to the earth. We were taught to look for the "heart," which must be gently removed and returned to the ground with its "head." That lesson stayed with us. Not just about harvesting. About relationship and reciprocity.

We teach the same. We know the plant's flower turns to seed and distributes itself. Still, we pass on the rituals of the old people. It was what they were shown and how they honored their ancestors. How we honor ours. And so forth.

We gather bitterroot each spring (March-May) in specific prairies across British Columbia and Montana. We prepare it simply. Cooked with sugar. Berry soups using bitterroot alongside serviceberries, huckleberries, and chokecherries.

Its scientific name, *rediviva*, means "brought back to life." Even when it seems to disappear during drought, bitterroot waits for the right conditions to return. **A lesson in resilience and trust.**

Health Benefits

Offers **exceptional nutritional density**; even small portions provide enough sustained energy to carry a person through an entire day of labor.

We use it in cough syrups and immune-strengthening infusions. Increases milk production in nursing mothers. Traditionally used for heart health and blood sugar management, conditions often connected in the body.

Habitat and Description

Produces striking **pink to white flowers** with around 15 petals. Its succulent leaves wither before blooming, and the flower appears to emerge directly from the earth.

Opens in sunlight and closes at night. Blooms March through June.

Thrives in arid grasslands with rocky, gravelly soils, sagebrush flats, open prairies, lower elevations.

Large-flowered Triteleia *(Triteleia grandiflora)*

(Edible / Spiritual / Practical)

Traditional Uses and Cultural Significance
Through knowledge holders and our own on-the-land tastings, we've come to know this plant. The deep, scaly corms are steamed or roasted, with a mouthfeel similar to maxa (glacier lily) and a very mild flavor.

We've observed Triteleia growing alongside camas and bitterroot, though it appears slightly later in the season, extending the root harvest and helping sustain families during transition times.

We eat and snack on the corms in season, and preserve some for teaching and later use.

Gatherers carried the corms, valuing them as portable sustenance that could be preserved. Used in food preparation to balance and stretch meals, they offered carbohydrates for sustained energy.

Health Benefits
The corms are **rich in carbohydrates**, making them a valuable **energy source** during gathering journeys and long travel days. The **young seed pods** are also prepared and consumed as a **potherb**.

Habitat and Description
Produces **funnel-shaped flowers** ranging from blue to white, arranged in umbel-like clusters atop smooth, leafless stems reaching up to 75 cm in height.

Grows from a deep, scaly corm and sends up two to three long, linear basal leaves. Blooms after other spring root foods have faded.

Thrives in grasslands, open woodlands, and forest clearings, preferring well-drained soils with seasonal moisture patterns.

Wild Licorice *(Glycyrrhiza lepidota)*

(Edible / Medicinal / Spiritual / Practical)

Traditional Uses and Cultural Significance
Wild Licorice offers gifts throughout its life cycle. The **roots** carry **distinctive sweetness** that complements other foods and serves as a **natural tooth cleaner**. For children, particularly during **teething**, a carefully cleaned piece of root brings both comfort and gentle medicinal support. In **early spring**, its **tender shoots** provide valuable nourishment when fresh greens are just beginning to emerge.

In our skincare formulations, we use Wild Licorice root in **solar-infused oils**. It addresses **eczema, sensitive skin, redness, and inflammation**.

Health Benefits
The roots contain glycyrrhizin, significantly sweeter than sugar and valued in traditional medicine. We prepare tea from the root to support respiratory health, aid digestion, and reduce fevers. In our teachings, this tea also plays a role in childbirth, particularly supporting delivery of the placenta.

We apply mashed leaves as poultices for wounds and skin irritation. Chewing the root helps relieve toothaches and sore throats while freshening breath.

Habitat and Description
Produces **yellowish-white flowers** in dense, stalked clusters. Compound leaves with eleven to nineteen pointed leaflets covered in fine glandular dots. Becomes sticky and strongly aromatic when mature.

Blooms May through August. Grows up to three feet tall with fibrous roots that emit sweet, anise-like aroma.

Found along streambanks, open grasslands, prairies, and disturbed areas.

Sticky Purple Geranium *(Geranium viscosissimum)*

(Edible / Medicinal / Practical)

Traditional Uses and Cultural Significance

We gather Sticky Purple Geranium each season because it is foundational to our skincare work. It appears in nearly every formulation we create: infused oils, creams, salves, lotions, and soaps. Through patient observation and attunement, we've learned it works synergistically with other plants. One is only as good as the company it keeps.

We use it for rosacea, acne scars, eczema, oily skin, and rashes: skin conditions that can affect confidence and daily life.

Health Benefits

Contains **natural astringents** that help **contract blood vessels**, making it reliable for **checking bleeding and supporting wound care**.

We prepare infusions from the leaves to ease colds and make gargles for sore throats. Traditional teachings include using both leaves and roots in washes to soothe sore eyes and in poultices for cuts, abrasions, and inflamed skin.

Particularly effective in **salves for chapped lips, cracked hands, and dry skin**.

Habitat and Description

Produces vibrant **pink to purple, saucer-shaped flowers** in open, branching clusters. **Deeply lobed, palmate leaves** covered in **sticky glandular hairs**.

Reaches **half a foot to three feet in height. Blooms May through July**.

Found in **ponderosa pine forests, northern juniper woodlands, and open meadows** from lowland zones to subalpine elevations. Prefers **drier grasslands and lightly shaded forest edges**.

ʔinq̓am, Prairie Crocus *(Anemone patens)*

(Medicinal / Spiritual / Practical)

Traditional Uses and Cultural Significance

Prairie Crocus, known as *ʔinq̓am* in our language, holds a special place in our early spring observations. We remember being drawn to its fine, silky hairs as children, watching tiny insects move across its petals. This is where we learned about food webs: insects pollinate, become food for predators, feed the cycle that keeps everything moving.

In our seasonal teachings, *ʔinq̓am* appears alongside bitterroot, between winter and spring. It is one of the first messengers of renewal, signaling that the land is waking and that it's time to begin observing, listening, and gathering again.

Medicinally, Prairie Crocus has long been used in treatments for rheumatism, neuralgia, and lung conditions. Our teachings emphasize caution and careful preparation, as its potency can be harmful if misused. In skilled hands, its medicine speaks to the strength of early spring plants: their ability to offer powerful healing after a long season of stillness and scarcity.

Health Benefits

Fresh leaves have been used in traditional medicine when **properly prepared** to address a range of conditions. **Poultices** made from crushed material have been applied to relieve **headaches and localized pain**.

Decoctions of the root have been used for **respiratory issues, including chronic lung conditions**. There are also teachings about using specific parts in carefully prepared treatments for **eye conditions such as cataracts**.

Habitat and Description

Produces soft **lavender to pale white blossoms** with five to eight petal-like sepals. Stems and finely divided leaves covered in silky, insulating hairs. Ranges from three to eighteen inches tall. Blooms March through May.

Found in open prairies, dry sandy soils, and lightly wooded areas with full sun to partial shade. Prefers well-drained, undisturbed soils and is adapted to cold, dry conditions.

Wiyu, Prickly Pear *(Opuntia fragilis)*

(Edible / Medicinal / Practical)

Traditional Uses and Cultural Significance

Our relationship with Prickly Pear, or Wiyu, began during bitterroot harvests, when we first encountered it the hard way: sacrificing more than one pair of shoes but gaining valuable teachings in return. Since then, this resilient cactus has become a familiar presence, playing a role in many of our seasonal tastings and handmade formulations.

The pads are edible when properly prepared, though the texture can be described as mucousy. Chilled or blended, they work well in smoothies where they lend body to other flavors without overpowering. The flavor is mild.

Traditional uses include treating burns, soothing inflammation, and assisting during childbirth. The plant's ability to reproduce vegetatively, sending out new life through its detachable pads, speaks to its adaptability and persistence. We use Prickly Pear in our body care products for its anti-inflammatory and antioxidant properties.

Health Benefits

The **pads and juice** contain potent anti-inflammatory and antioxidant compounds. We use these in our salves, creams, and seasonal body care infusions.

Traditional teachings include using poultices made from the plant's inner gel to relieve skin irritations, rheumatism, and surface wounds. Medicinally, Wiyu supports metabolic health, recognized for its ability to lower cholesterol, balance blood sugar, and regulate inflammation.

Habitat and Description

Produces bold **yellow flowers, three to five centimeters in diameter**, blooming May through July. Low-growing, mat-forming structure with jointed stems and elliptical to rounded pads measuring two to five centimeters. Pads armed with clusters of three to seven sharp, barbed spines. Develops pear-shaped fruits following bloom.

Found in **dry environments** such as deserts, open grasslands, prairies, and sun-exposed slopes. Prefers sandy, well-drained soils at low to mid elevations.

Part Five: Summer

Walking Through Summer

"The land offers abundance, teaching us gratitude and careful selection. Our ancestors harvested with intention, and now we carry their discernment forward, knowing that abundance is not about taking more, but about honoring what is given."

Summer arrives the way Ayla knows it will: not by calendar, but by grasshoppers. When they appear, thick in the grass and clinging to wildflowers, she knows the huckleberries are coming. The bears know too. We're all watching the same signs, listening to the same language.

Each ripening berry and unfurling petal is a storyteller, carrying ancestral teachings of reciprocity, stewardship, and gratitude.

Before we walk deeper into the richness of ʔaqsukutnamu, pause for a moment. What sensations awaken in your body when you think of summer? What relationships feel fuller, more alive? This way of noticing, of feeling the season as teacher, is the root of traditional understanding. **True abundance lives not only in what we gather, but in how we receive.**

Summer Solstice: The Gift of Light

The Summer Solstice: when light is fullest, when we see differently. Not because the day is longer, but because we shift.

We become warmer. Sometimes too hot. We find pleasure in simple things: sprinklers, lakes, ice cream. **We are fully present, open, aware, receptive.**

Nothing changes externally. Same hours. Same minutes. But something shifts internally. **This is the gift of light: not more time, but presence. Not duration, but awareness.**

The light doesn't linger. It simply is. Our light. The earth's light. All beings see it, feel it, grow from it.

The plants teach us this. Flowers throwing themselves open. Berries beginning their slow sweetening. Leaves concentrating their medicine. They are in full bloom.

So are we. Everything we worked on beneath the surface in spring now shows itself. This is our inflorescence. We are walking through our own seasonal change, arriving at fullness alongside the plants.

This is the height of abundance, and abundance carries responsibility.

Not duty or obligation, but attention. **Where do we place our time? Who do we show up for? What practices do we choose? What**

do we gift freely, and to whom?

Responsibility is knowing our pace. Moving at the rhythm that serves what matters: family, land, those closest to us. **We cannot give our attention everywhere. We choose where it goes.**

Stand in this fullness and the core principles of our plant relationships come into focus:

Discernment in Abundance

Summer brings richness, but abundance is not permission to take without limit. We choose thoughtfully: which plants to harvest, which to leave for our wild relatives, and which to protect for future generations. This is how we honor balance.

Peak Medicine and Timing

At solstice, many plants reach their medicinal prime. Flowers open fully, releasing potent scent and healing essence. Leaves concentrate their oils and medicine. Berries begin their sweetening.

We harvest not just what is available, but what is ready. **Timing is everything.** One always arrives on time when moving at their own pace.

Honoring the Sun's Gifts

Every plant carries the sun's energy in its cells. Through photosynthesis, our green relatives transform golden rays into nourishment and medicine. When we gather, we harvest light itself, stored in form for seasons to come.

Community Connection

Summer is a time of collective work. Families and communities gather, prepare, and preserve the land's abundance. These are moments of laughter, learning, and deepening kinship with each other and with the plants.

The Solstice is a threshold: a moment to pause, reflect, and move forward with intention. Even in summer's generosity, we gather with respect, take only what we need, and give thanks. In this way, we carry the sun's gifts with us, preparing body and spirit.

Summer Solstice Prayer

Prayer of Abundance, Keepers of the Seasons

Creator, we thank You for this season of light, for the fullness that surrounds us. We give thanks for the warmth that nourishes the soil, for the bees and birds who carry prayers between blossoms.

May we remember that abundance is not for hoarding, but for sharing. May our words, actions, and hearts reflect the generosity of the sun.

Reflection: Living in Relationship

Summer invites us to live in relationship. Not scattered, but intentional.

This season is not only about growth, but about tending. **And tending requires inventory.** Where are we placing our attention? What are we growing? Does it still serve our vision, our family, the greater good?

Inventory keeps us humble. It keeps us grateful. It lets us walk in integrity.

The natural world shows us this. Wildfires sometimes leave landscapes bare, but not barren. Floods carve new waterways. Wind removes debris. **What looks like ending is often preparation.** Even in summer's fullness, the land clears what doesn't serve.

Growth humbles ego. When we take inventory, we see what we're actually tending versus what we think we're tending. We notice where our time goes, who we show up for, what practices we've let slip.

Inventory can recur. It is a thinking point. A pause. It lets us adjust before patterns become problems.

When what we put out to the world comes back as abundance, happiness, joy, love, we truly see the work of our inventory. We're tending what matters. And tending becomes reciprocal. What we care for, cares for us back. Gift. Abundance.

We have slowed enough to take it for what it is.

Summer teaches us that abundance isn't about having more. It's about knowing what matters, taking inventory, and tending it with full presence.

Gathering With Awareness: Walking In Light

Growth humbles ego. When we take inventory, we see what we're actually tending versus what we think we're tending. We notice where our time goes, who we show up for, what practices we've let slip.

Inventory recurs. It is a thinking point. A pause. It lets us adjust before patterns become problems.

When what we put out to the world comes back in abundance: happiness, joy, love, we truly see the work of our inventory. We're tending what matters. And tending becomes reciprocal. What we care for, cares for us back. Gift. Abundance.

We have slowed enough to take it for what it is.

Summer teaches us that abundance isn't about having more. It's about knowing what matters, taking inventory, and tending it with

full presence.

All it took was growing. Growth humbled ego. We set intention. We walk in integrity. We give ourselves permission to protect our spirit, to be present, to stay willing: to learn, to laugh, to love, to belong again.

Protocol is permission we give ourselves. Humility is knowing enough to show up and keep learning. Gratitude is being grateful for a new day.

This is what it means to walk in light: participating in life.

In our family, this is a timeless season. To notice what Ayla knows about phenology, we had to be present. **That's what lets us see what really matters.**

Even in her pool-splashing, trampoline-bouncing joy, she tracks ripening by watching the bugs, birds, and animals gathering to sweetness. She knows the weather is turning right for huckleberries when the grasshoppers arrive. **One relationship reveals many.** Summer's abundance is announced by the plants and all who circle them.

This is the language of the plants. Not observation. Participation.

When we show up in light, we gift light and purpose.

The youth become our teachers. They point out places we might have missed, remind us to slow down, ask questions that make us think deeper about why we do what we do.

This is how knowledge stays alive: through hands that touch the same berries, through eyes that learn to see the same signs, through families who remember together. For those reconnecting after separation, this is the work. Showing up. Learning alongside children. Letting them teach you what they notice.

And in summer, light invites us back quickly. Back to swimming, playing, laughing, loving. Back to picking berries to eat fresh, to preserve, to have stories about. Back to the simple abundance of being here, together, present.

There is vast abundance when we harvest with awareness. We attune to other harvesters and wild relatives. Notice where pickers have been, where animals have eaten, and adjust. This is not about rushing to beat others. It is about presence.

> *"We come to gather your gifts alongside our relatives. We take some and leave many, knowing others rely on you too: bears, birds, bugs, and all our wild kin. We thank you for your generosity and ask that our harvesting helps you return next season, strong, rooted, and plentiful."*

This is ceremony. Harvesting as relationship. Abundance as shared responsibility. **Stewardship is not control or ownership. It is respect, reciprocity, and return.**

Summer's Botanical Gifts

For those who cannot. For those just remembering. For those yet to come.

Our plant relatives reveal their fullest medicines in summer. Many offer different gifts across the seasons: tender leaves in spring, vibrant flowers in summer, potent seeds in fall, healing roots in winter. Each part carries its own wisdom, story, and relationship to our bodies and spirits.

Mid-Summer Gathering

Flowers at peak bloom (for food, medicine, and ceremony)

Berries as they ripen (each variety following its own sweet timing)

Leafy greens (harvested before they bolt or turn bitter)

Plants for drying and long-term storage

Optimal Harvesting Times

Flowers: mid-morning after the dew lifts, before full heat

Berries: fully ripe yet firm, gather in stages as they mature

Medicinal leaves: often before flowering, some strongest in bloom

Seeds: as they ripen and firm, before they shatter and scatter

Traditional Teaching

Throughout summer we are always looking ahead.

Not in anxiety. Just in knowing. **Knowing that others will call on us for things they may have missed.** We watch for buckbrush, Trapper's Tea, and rosehips.

How do we make the most of this time and our gifts? We appreciate what we have, who we have.

Deep kinship does not follow linear time. It spirals through giving and receiving, asking and listening, moving with the rhythms that hold us all.

What happens when summer's expected abundance is disrupted? When wildfire smoke dulls the sky and drought withers berries on the vine? These are the times when relationship is tested, when ceremony becomes essential, and when reciprocity is called to its deepest expression.

To understand this more fully, we turn to story.

Ka'ski'in numa

It was one of the hottest summers to ever hit the valley, smoke blanketed the sky, the air was thick, and ash fell like snow. There was little moisture in the earth, everything was dry, and plants wilted. Mi¢qaqas (chickadee) flew through the trees trying to find a place to rest. While flying, he could hear something in the distance and followed the sound. He flew through some trees and down towards a small camp. There was a small hut made of woven cattails. And out behind the hut, Titi was tending to some berries she just finished picking. As he flew nearer, he could hear the old titi singing her song to Numa (thunder). Hey, ya, hey, ya, ho, hey, ya, hey, ya, hey, ka?s ki?in numa, hey, ya, hey, ya, hey, hey, ya, hey ka?s ki?in numa. Mi¢qaqas heard her singing and wished he could do something for her. He knew the words to her song and went to seek Numa. Mi¢qaqas flew to the end of the valley and high into the mountains. He could barely see where he was going but he listened to the far away grumblings that guided him to his destination. Up high in the mountain where the air is thin and the ground is made of shale, he saw Numa, grumbling and making his arrows. "Mi¢qaqas, qapsin kin?u?t?" grumbled Numa. "Ah, we haven't seen you around and we were getting worried about you", said Mi¢qaqas. "Is that so? Well, I can tell you I am fine and have been here where I always am". "Yes, Numa, and I am glad I found you, because that old titi down there is wondering about your whereabouts". "Hmmmmm, I knew there was something more. No one just pays me a visit without wanting something. So, you're saying she sent you to get something from me?" "No, no, I heard her singing a song, praying for rain and for the fires to be put out. It's been so hot and so smoky, and the people are having a hard time preparing for the next season". "My arrows and my ?awumu bring rain and winds. I can do this for the people". "They and we would be very grateful for your gift, Numa". "BUT you must bring a message to that old titi. her people have lost their way, so she is to hold three meals. Two at her place and the third will be a feast. She will know where to have it, and her people will feast with her. They will sing, and they will pray, and they will eat good. When she is done holding these meals, I will bring the people their rain". So, with this news, Mi¢qaqas went on his way to see the old titi. Titi was still outside her hut, singing and tending to her berries. "Ki?suk kyukyit, titi". "Oh, ki?suk kyukyit, Mi¢qaqas, how are you today"? I am doing good, better after paying a visit to Numa. I heard you singing earlier". "Yes, the smoke and fires have made life difficult down here, even more so since I live on my own and have to do most everything myself". "Well, I told Numa about your song and prayers, he said he

he can help. But he wants you to do something first. You must hold two meals here at your house and then a feast on the third day. After you have completed these tasks, he will bring rain to put out the fires and wind to blow away the smoke." "Well, I have been busy gathering the berries, fishing and hunting, so I do have enough to have three meals". "You also have to invite your people, titi". "Ah, that won't be too hard. I can let them know when I go to fetch water this evening". And with that, Mi¢qaqas flew off. Titi finished cleaning her berries and grabbed her water container. She was feeling good from the news she heard today, and her heart was happy. On her way to get water, she saw some relatives "I'm having a meal at my house tomorrow. You should come and let the others know they are invited so we can eat together". After she was done letting her people know and gathering her water. She went home and took out the berries she was cleaning. "I'm glad for the things my family taught me," she thought, as she went to her food cache and took out some dried roots. *I can make some berry soup, with this dried bitterroot, and we will have fresh huckleberries and we will eat on this pemmican I have.* She cooked into the night and sang the songs her titi taught her. She was smiling and happy; she knew she was going to sleep well.

  The next day, Titi was so excited for the meal she was going to share that she was up with the sun. She sang and sang, thinking of the relatives and friends she was going to see today. Titi and her people haven't gathered in a long time, and she missed everyone she knew. She was feeling so grateful for the gift she was going to be sharing with everyone. Her berry soup tasted like her titis, and the fresh huckleberries shared their magic in every bite, the pemmican reminded her of the time she spent with her dad and uncles, every food had a memory, and every memory made her heart smile. She cleaned her house and living area and set out the food. Soon there was an old friend. Her niece and children made their way to her house. A couple more visitors joined, and they were ready to eat. "I am glad that you all came for this meal today. We have been struggling with all this smoke and hot weather. I have been praying for rain, but I also pray for you, my friends and family, that you have food and shelter, that you have friendship and people to help you. I am sharing these berries and food that I have prepared. I have gone on many trips to the mountains alone, no one helps me out, I have nephews, and nieces, but no one helps me. I climb high and am gone all day, I pick and gather these foods alone, but I love – what I do, and I love every one of you and that's why I am happy to open my house and share my food for this meal". After titi shared her words, they all took some food. They ate and laughed and shared some good conversation. After the food was gone and everyone was fed, Titi told them she would be sharing another meal the next day.

      Titi woke to the birds chirping and singing their morning song. She woke even happier knowing that she would be able to share more laughs and stories with her friends and family. She was excited to know she would see more of her grand nieces and nephews, that she would visit with old friends, and that they would eat well. One by one, her family and friends showed up, she saw the people from yesterday and again a few more new faces joined them to eat. Titi started off "I am glad that you all came for this meal today. We haven't celebrated or gathered in a long time, we've struggled with smoke and fires, and we've struggled to gather as friends and family. I want you to know I have been praying for rain, but I also pray for you, my friends and family, that you have food and shelter, that you have friendship and people to help you. I am sharing this Salmon and food that I have prepared. I have gone on many trips to the river to catch salmon. They are big fish, heavy fish I am not as strong as I used to be and I catch these fish alone, no one helps me out, I have nephews, and nieces, but no one helps me. I travel far and through rough waters and I am gone all day. I fish and pick and gather these foods alone, but I love, what I do, and I love every one of you and that's why I am happy to open my house and share my food for this meal". The children ate first today as Titi wanted the people to know the importance of caring for our children and that it is important to guide them and provide knowledge. To make sure they are fed. After everyone was full and happy, they gathered their things and started to leave for home. Titi thanked everyone for coming and started to prepare things for the next day. Titi took everything from her food cache and along with her fresh deer meat and readied it for the next day. She looked around her house and thought of the meals she prepared this week, she thought of the little faces, the new faces and the old faces, she could hear the laughs and the happy conversations, she was so grateful for the way creator answered her prayers, she knew this week was one of her greatest gifts.

      The next morning, titi woke from a dream of the waterfalls, she dreamt of a beautiful spot on the water's edge that her late husband used to take her to and she knew this was where she would have her feast. She gathered everything she prepared and started to make her way to the falls. She stopped at the houses of her previous dinner guests and told them she would be having the feast at the falls. She told them to let the rest of their people know and that they were all invited. She saw a few more people along the way and let them know she was heading to the falls to host a feast. She struggled to carry everything, but persevered. Being careful not to lose anything along the way. She made a few stops along her way but made sure to drink water and to stay cool during her trip. She

finally made it to the falls late in the morning. She started to dig a small pit and built a fire. She gathered some water and set out her foods. She was able to pit cook some deer, smoked some of her meats. She had many roots and bulbs that would cook with bones to make broth. She had fresh berries. Titi was able to feed all her people, and she did, as one by one everyone from the village started to show up. The people gathered and they waited for Titi to start… "Hello everyone, I am so, so, so glad that you all came for this feast today. This spot we are eating is special to me, and today it is special to our people. We haven't gathered to celebrate, or to even just be together in a long time. This year we have been struggling with all this smoke and hot weather. I have been praying for rain, but I pray mostly for you, my friends and family, that you have food and shelter, that you are all safe, that you have friendship and people to help you and that you are all happy and find your way in life. Today I am sharing all my food with you these berries, this fish, this deer. Everything that I have prepared. I have gotten on my own. I have taken many trips to the mountains alone, I've caught many heavy salmon alone, and I hunted, gutted, and dressed this deer alone. No one helps me out, I have nephews, and nieces, but no one helps me. I climb high and am gone all day, I pick and gather these foods alone, I hunt alone, and I cooked alone. But I love what I do, and I love every one of you and that is why I am happy to open my heart to you and I share my food for this feast. I prayed that the heat and fires would be gone, Mi¢qaqas told me he brought my prayers to Numa, and that there would be rain after this feast. So, let's eat, and hope that what he said is true". So, the people ate, and ate, and ate. Titi was eating and enjoying the energy from her people, her heart was full of happiness and gratitude. She got up and looked happily at everyone, she looked at the water and the falls and a song entered her heart. "Everyone, I am going to sing a song. I have my drum with me, I made this drum from the hide of the deer I hunted, no one helped me skin the deer, or tan the hide. I have nieces, nephews and other family who could have helped me, but I did it on my own. I am going to sing and share with you all, because I love each and every one of you. We will sing and we will be grateful for today and we will pray for Numa to bring the rain". Titi, rose from her chair and banged her drum, she started to sing. She sang and sang until everyone was singing with her. She looked to the sky praying for the rain. She walked up the path beside the waterfall, her heart filled with happiness. She could hear the singing and she could feel the air changing. Tears began to roll down Titi's cheeks, as she got closer to the top of the falls. She stopped and looked down to all the happy faces, all the new faces and all the old faces. She was happy to see them gathered and singing together, praying together, being together. The singing was louder, and she banged her drum harder. She looked atop the trees and could see Numa moving in with the clouds. He gave her a nod and the tears flowed harder. She could hear Numa whispering to her through the growl of the waterfall. She looked to the falls and saw an old pathway to the top. She kept singing and started to walk towards the path, following the whisper, his guidance. She could still hear her people singing as she walked higher up the falls. She looked down and saw the people looking at her singing, smiling, and praying hard. The sound of the falls muffled the singing, muffled the sound of her drum, but she banged hard and sang even harder. She looked at the people and happiness filled her heart. She sang and sang and drummed and drummed. She had tears running down her cheeks. She was finally at the top of the falls, her heart full of happiness and tears streaming down her cheeks. She paused for a moment, took a deep breath, and jumped.

Her drum echoed through the valley and the people continued to sing. Titi felt herself being lifted as Numa carried her across the valley. He carried her past the village, and he carried her over the falls. Her tears raining on the lands and the people she loved. Her song and her words of love whispered out of the falls. Hearing her words of love dancing out of the water, a feeling of awe, love, and respect entered the hearts of the people. They began to understand sacrifice and the importance of connection to family and all living things.

Black Medick *(Medicago lupulina)*

(Edible / Medicinal)

Traditional Uses and Cultural Significance

Black Medick, though a non-native plant, has found its way into our summer gathering practices. Its presence often marks disturbed soil, signaling how landscapes have shifted over time. While not traditionally part of Indigenous foodways, we've explored its offerings: cooking the leaves, parching the seeds, grinding them into a fine powder, and brewing them into tea.

This plant has become a quiet teacher. It reminds us that knowledge is not static. As ecosystems change, so do the relationships we form. Black Medick shows us how to adapt, how to listen, and how to find meaning in unexpected places. It speaks to resilience, not just in land, but in culture and learning.

Health Benefits

Some of our most meaningful plant teachings come through unexpected sources. *Dreams, stories, or quiet observations passed on by elders.* Through them, we've learned to value plants like Black Medick **not just for their origin, but for their offering**.

While western science identifies **antibacterial and mild analgesic properties** in its extracts, our understanding of this plant deepens through *lived experience*. It has supported us during **active summer months**, when scrapes, inflammation, and small injuries call for gentle care. **What it offers is not loud, but steady.**

Habitat and Description

Small **yellow flowers (2–3 mm)** form dense, rounded clusters **(5–10 mm)** of **10–35 blooms** that nod gently, blooming **May through August**. **Trifoliate leaves** with toothed margins on the upper half of each leaflet. Distinctive **black, kidney-shaped seed pods** with veined surfaces mature later in the season, these are the seeds we parch and grind.

Often found along **roadsides, fields, meadows, and disturbed grasslands**, from valleys to plains. Grows in a **sprawling to ascending form**, reaching **10–45 cm in height**. Its ability to thrive in disrupted areas often signals **human presence and land impact**.

sq̓umu, Saskatoon berry
(Amelanchier alnifolia)

(Edible / Medicinal / Practical)

Traditional Uses and Cultural Significance
Sq̓umu holds a special place in our summer gathering traditions. Bears feast on these berries to prepare for winter, just as we harvest them for immediate enjoyment and winter storage.

We remember a particularly hot summer day coming upon a tree heavy with ripe berries. After eating handful after handful, we discovered their natural fermentation: the sugars and heat creating a slightly intoxicating effect that left us with both nourishment and laughter.

We dry the berries, mix them into pemmican, and value them for their iron-rich nourishment, which builds blood and strength. Both *sq̓umu* and the junipers respond well to controlled burns, a practice used by our ancestors, which now proves valuable for both stimulating growth and mitigating disease.

We've been able to enjoy this treat in pies, bitterroot soup, and berry mixes with whipped cream or ice cream. It also makes quite the impression in one of our prized wildberry preserves: huckleberry, chokecherry, serviceberry, and foam berry.

Health Benefits
The fruits are a rich source of **iron and antioxidants.** We make **decoctions of the juice** as a **digestive aid** and **gentle laxative.** *Root decoctions* have been used to address **colds, fevers,** and **respiratory infections,** while *bark preparations* are part of our **women's health knowledge**. Especially, helpful for **regulating menstrual cycles after childbirth.**

Habitat and Description
Produces clusters of **showy white flowers** with *five oblong petals*, blooming **April through June.** Develops **round, purple-black fruits** with a *sweet, slightly almond-like flavor.* Alternate, **oval-shaped leaves** with *sharply toothed edges.* Grows as a **deciduous shrub** reaching *1–3 meters tall.* Thrives in **open woods, forest edges, and meadows** from valleys to subalpine regions. We've observed **increasing susceptibility to rust**, especially in areas with **conifer cover.**

Ka¢ɬaquɬaqpi·k, Thimbleberry
(Rubus parviflorus)

(Edible / Medicinal / Practical)
Traditional Uses and Cultural Significance
Ka¢ɬaquɬaqpi·k doesn't demand attention with sweetness like other berries, but it stays with you. Its soft, dry fruit carries substance. It brings body to what we make: our jams, sauces, and shared dishes, adding depth where others bring brightness.

Ayla is often the first to spot them, popping thimbleberries into her mouth while scouting for huckleberries. In our family, that moment has become a signal: huckleberry season is near.

We don't just gather the berries. The tender spring shoots are peeled and eaten raw, a once-common seasonal food that still surprises us with its softness. The broad, velvety leaves have lined our baskets, protected our food, and reminded us that some plants give with ease.

Health Benefits
The **leaves** are used in **blood-tonic teas**, especially helpful for **nausea or prolonged menstruation**. We've used **poultices of dried powdered leaves** for **wounds and burns**, and **fresh leaves rubbed on skin** to calm **pimples**.

Berries provide **vitamin C**, supporting the immune system, while **root decoctions** are used for **skin conditions** and as a gentle **astringent**.

Habitat and Description
Blooms **May through July** with large, showy **white flowers** bearing **five broad petals** in open clusters. **Maple-like leaves** with **heart-shaped bases** are distinctively **soft to the touch, velvety and thornless**.

Growing **2–10 feet tall**, the **thornless stems** make this one of the most generous plants to harvest from.

Thrives in **moist environments: open forests, thickets, avalanche paths, and patchy woodlands**. Spreads through **underground rhizomes**, forming **dense stands** in disturbed areas.

ʼkitʼquǂkaǂmaxaka, Yarrow *(Achillea millefolium)*

(Edible / Medicinal / Spiritual / Practical)

Traditional Uses and Cultural Significance

Yarrow is one of those plants that lives in our hearts, for all the right reasons. It appears when needed, a quiet presence along riverbanks and disturbed edges. We remember days fishing and swimming, swarmed by mosquitoes, when our parents taught us to rub yarrow on our skin. It worked. Another time, after stepping on a wasp, yarrow mixed with mud soothed the sting: that blend of cool earth and bitter plant somehow making pain bearable.

We carry a story from a knowledge holder from Yaqan Nukiy, who in the late '90s sought a plant to help with diabetes and worsening vision. Drinking yarrow tea in quantity, he later laughed, "Well, it didn't help my diabetes… but the mosquitoes sure stayed away from me that year." His medicine, it turned out, was Devil's Club. This is how plant knowledge lives: through story, trial, humor, and remembered advice.

Health Benefits

Yarrow has long been trusted for its **wound care**. Our parents and grandparents taught us how quickly it closes a cut, a gift the plant still carries. Science later described alkaloids behind this action, but in our families **the teaching is simple: yarrow stops the bleeding.**

Teas are remembered for easing **colds, fevers, and infections**, offering steady, bitter medicine that supports the body through illness. For **women's wellness**, a **cool steep of young leaves** helps with **menstrual cramps and heavy bleeding.** These teachings live through story and repeated use.

Habitat and Description

Blooms **May through September**, producing **small white flowers (occasionally pinkish)** with **5–12 rays** arranged in **flat-topped clusters (2–15 cm across). Erect stems reach 6–60 cm in height. Finely divided, feathery leaves** grow alternately along the stem, giving a **fern-like appearance**. An **aromatic perennial** spreading through resilient rhizomes. Thrives in **diverse environments from grasslands and meadows to open forests and stream banks**. Often appearing in **disturbed areas** like roadsides, urban edges, places where the earth has been opened.

Kyan‡ak‡iqu‡aqpik, Heart-leafed Arnica *(Arnica cordifolia)*

(Edible / Medicinal / Spiritual / Practical)

Traditional Uses and Cultural Significance

This is one of our pre-warmth gatherings, collected before the heat of summer settles in, when the plant's medicine is most concentrated. Its bright yellow flowers become the foundation of many seasonal offerings, transforming into infused oils that find their way into our salves and healing blends. Arnica plays an important role in our traditional salves, an alternative to lotions or roll-on oils. It works alongside cottonwood bud, sweetgrass, and other solar-infused oils. We formulate based on ailment and intention, addressing rashes, eczema, dry scalp, arthritis, and spiritual grounding.

We know this plant through careful touch and timing. We follow the moon's cycle when preparing arnica oil, filling glass jars with dried flowers, covering them with oil, and placing them in warm, dark places to steep. The process becomes its own form of ceremony: shaking the jars every few days, straining through cheesecloth, pressing out every last drop of medicine. We've learned to respect its power. Arnica is used only on unbroken skin, reminding us that some medicines work best from the outside in. Its strength asks for precision, care, and timing.

Health Benefits

Arnica is a potent **anti-inflammatory and analgesic**, especially when used **topically**. We prepare it as **poultices, salves, and infused oils** to relieve **bruises, sprains, muscle pain, and swelling**. Its **sesquiterpene lactones and flavonoids** are responsible for its deep cellular healing and stimulation of blood flow.

Internal use is unsafe and requires extreme caution. We honor this plant's potency by respecting its boundaries. It is **medicine for the surface, for the muscle, not the bloodstream**.

Habitat and Description

Produces showy, **daisy-like yellow flowers** with golden disc and ray florets, blooming from **spring to early summer**. Growing up to **2 feet tall** from **spreading rhizomes**, it features **heart-shaped basal leaves** that are finely toothed and long-petioled. Erect stems often bearing **one or more flower heads per plant**. Thrives in **coniferous forests, mountain meadows, and subalpine regions**, growing at elevations between **3,500–10,000 feet**. **Resprouts after wildfire**.

Muk, Bunchberry *(Cornus canadensis)*

(Edible / Medicinal / Spiritual)

Traditional Uses and Cultural Significance

Bunchberry has reshaped our life in profound ways, especially around pain and relaxation. Debilitating tension headaches that started in grade school, so excruciating at times that daily things like eating, going to school, playing, just enjoying life became impossible. After developing hives from overusing ibuprofen, the search for relief led first to violets, then nettles, and finally to bunchberry through patient observation and love.

This plant has become a gift we lean on: pleasant in tea, powerful when smoked with other medicines, and steady in preventing and relieving pain.

Through years of observation and learning, we've come to understand its kinship with red-osier dogwood. Both share qualities that support relaxation and pain management, teachings that have been affirmed through experience, story, and later study.

For us, bunchberry is a godsend. It finally gifted actual measurable relief.

Health Benefits

The **leaves and stems** carry teachings for easing **aches, pains, and tension**. **Teas** have supported us through **kidney and lung ailments, coughs, and fevers**. A strong **decoction** has served as an **eyewash**, while **root preparations** were once given for **infant colic**.

The **berries**, rich in **pectin**, offer gentle **digestive support**. They have a **refreshing pop, not too mealy**.

Habitat and Description

Bunchberry produces **small flowers surrounded by four large white bracts** in late spring. It grows **close to the earth. Up to 25 cm tall**, with **whorls of broad, oval leaves**.

By late summer, **clusters of bright red berries** signal their presence, standing out against the forest floor.

Thrives in **cool, moist environments: coniferous forests, thickets, damp clearings, and shady, humus-rich soils**. Often forms **dense groundcover**, weaving itself like a living blanket through our territories.

Q̓uɬwa, Wood's Rose: petals *(Rosa woodsii)*

(Edible / Medicinal / Spiritual / Practical)
Traditional Uses and Cultural Significance
Q̓uɬwa is a deeply respected spiritual plant in our families. After the death of a loved one, we use rose to wash ourselves, clean the house, and cleanse the belongings of those who have passed. This plant guards the spirit and cleanses what doesn't belong: heaviness, grief, or energies that no longer serve us.

This rose has been central to our medicine work. The grandmothers taught us how to gather the petals, prepare infused oils, and use rose in ceremony and healing. They showed us when to harvest, how to work with the plant respectfully, what it heals. The flower is beautiful and protected by thorns, yet gentle enough for skin and scent. Petals tucked in a pillow bring good rest. The memory of those teachers lives in that scent, in the knowledge they passed down through their hands.

Gathering petals for infused oils became both ritual and practice, something we carry yearly that later grew into the skincare line itself. Rose is a star ingredient in many of our formulas. We work with different roses from the Rosaceae family: Wood's rose, crabapple blossoms, and others, sometimes sourcing concentrated rose oil or combining types to create the right blend for skin healing. The seasonal cycle offers lessons in continuity: petals that soften and soothe, dropping gracefully to make way for hips gathered in autumn for winter medicine.

Health Benefits
Rose petals are steeped as tea to ease sore throats, calm the stomach, and settle the nervous system. Baths or washes made with petals soothe irritated skin and offer emotional grounding after hardship. Petals are also used in baby washes and eye compresses for their gentleness. **Rosehips**, bright and tart, provide **vitamin C** and **strengthen immunity** during winter months, while **roots and stems** serve as reliable **astringents**.

Habitat and Description
Dry rocky slopes, moist streambanks, grasslands, and subalpine forests. It grows dense thorny stems reaching **1–2 meters tall**. Fragrant flowers, soft pink to deep rose, bloom in late spring and early summer. Compound leaves with 5–9 serrated leaflets.

Yuk, Elderberry *(Sambucus cerulea)*

(Edible / Medicinal / Spiritual / Practical)

Traditional Uses and Cultural Significance

Yuk carries heart memory: bittersweet, protective, and enduring. Some of our most treasured plant-sharing videos capture time spent with Grandma Jenny during the early days of COVID. Together we made winter syrup, elderberry at its core, blended with many valued plant allies.

But the real medicine wasn't just in the jar. It was in the way she was with us. She sang, she told stories, she shared space with her sister, she laughed, she danced with Ayla. Every gesture was intentional, every moment infused with presence.

That teaching has stayed with us: medicine is not only what is combined, but how it is carried and gifted. Elderberry became the anchor, but the deeper gift was learning that healing lives in relationship, in the joy and care of being together, in the way song, laughter, and intention transform a simple preparation into ceremony.

In spring, our family make savoury Elderberry blossom fritters, beautiful with huckleberry syrup and powdered sugar.

Health Benefits

Ripe, blue-purple berries (always cooked) are rich in **vitamin C and antioxidants**, supporting **immune strength and respiratory health**. Syrups and decoctions made from berries help prevent and ease seasonal illness.

Flower teas break fevers, ease colds, and soothe the lungs, while bark preparations, used with care, can reduce pain and swelling.

We hold firmly to the teaching that elderberry's gifts are fully realized only when the plant is approached properly: ripe berries, cooked well, and never parts known to be toxic. Don't eat raw berries, they are known to cause nausea, vomiting, and digestive upset.

Habitat and Description

Grows as large shrub or small tree, reaching up to 30 feet. Cream-colored flowers bloom in broad, flat clusters from May through July, giving way to **waxy blue-purple berries.**

Found along streams, rocky slopes, and riparian edges, thrives from low valleys to high elevations around 3,000 meters. Prefers moist, well-drained soils but endures drier, open sites.

¢aqawuʔk, Kinnikinnick
(Arctostaphylos uva-ursi)

(Edible / Medicinal / Spiritual / Practical)

Traditional Uses and Cultural Significance

¢aqawuʔk has lived with our families for generations. Our relationship with it began through pipe smoke blends, where the leaves provide both physical and spiritual cleansing. It remains one of our most trusted ceremonial allies, grounding and clearing in ways that tobacco alone cannot.

Early memories with kinnikinnick are playful. As children walking through the forest, always drawn to the clusters of bright red berries. Each time asking if they were edible, the answer came with a smile: "The chipmunks eat them. They're not very good... just chipmunk food. But you can try." The berries had a mealy texture and little flavor.

Over time we learned that, like popcorn, the berries can be heated in oil until they pop, then seasoned with salt or other flavors. What looked like bland chipmunk food became something we could enjoy.

The leaves hold medicine. Harvested in early autumn, they are prepared into teas for kidney and bladder health, or dried for ceremonial smoking mixtures that cleanse both body and spirit. The roots also hold medicine and components for dye.

Health Benefits

The leaves contain **arbutin and tannins**, giving them **antibacterial and astringent properties**. Used for urinary tract infections, kidney support, and bladder health, valued as diuretics and anti-inflammatory medicine. Poultices treat rashes, burns, and skin sores, while teas are prepared as eyewashes or mouth rinses for cankers. **Not recommended during pregnancy,** and best taken in moderation over short durations.

Habitat and Description

An **evergreen** trailing shrub grows up to 20 cm tall, spreading slowly into dense mats across dry, sandy, or rocky soils. Small, leathery dark-green leaves persist year-round, while delicate, **urn-shaped pink flowers** bloom in clusters from **April** through **June**. By summer and fall, bright red berries appear. Found from lowland valleys to alpine slopes.

ʔa·kɬaɬku, Bear-grass *(Xerophyllum tenax)*

(Medicinal / Practical / Spiritual)

Traditional Uses and Cultural Significance
ʔa·kɬaɬku has been part of our landscape for as long as memory goes back. This is a plant we sit near when reflecting, taking personal inventory, being grateful, just resting, journaling, being mindful, connecting to our senses. We've found places to rest where it grows thick in the forest.

The tough, grass-like leaves were traditionally soaked, split, and woven into mats, baskets, and grass skirts by those who came before us. Some of that knowledge came through grandparents, some through written records, some through watching the plant itself.

The stalks make perfect spears and whips when children play. The plant blooms spectacularly, but only every 5-7 years. We've been privileged to see full white mountainscapes when many are in bloom.

Health Benefits
The **roots** hold **astringent qualities** and are used to **stop bleeding**. Chewed root poultices treat wounds, sprains, and injuries, while **decoctions** serve as washes for broken limbs and sore eyes. When washed, the roots create a **gentle lather**, offering both **cleansing and healing properties**.

Habitat and Description
Grows in **dense clumps** of **long, tough, evergreen leaves** from woody rhizomes. From May through August, sends up tall stalks reaching up to 1.5 meters, crowned with dense, fragrant clusters of small white flowers. Blooms are infrequent, appearing every 5–7 years.

A **fire-adapted species**, thrives in **open woods and subalpine meadows**, from **sea level to 2,700 meters**, preferring **well-drained soils**.

Northern Bedstraw *(Galium boreale)*

(Edible / Medicinal / Practical)

Traditional Uses and Cultural Significance
Northern Bedstraw was gathered for bedding: its sweet vanilla scent made sleeping places comfortable. We still notice that fragrance when we come across it.

Young leaves have been used as emergency food, and roasted seeds serve as a coffee substitute, though in moderation to avoid irritation. The roots produce red dye for fabric and crafts. Our knowledge keepers, seeing the formulations we create for acne, eczema, and psoriasis, have directed us to many plants to learn from. A few of them shared that bedstraw was relatively effective in treating different skin conditions and ailments.

Health Benefits
Hot plant compresses stop bleeding and reduce swelling. Leaf and root teas aid weight loss by increasing perspiration and urination. Applied to skin, **plant juice** soothes **sunburn and insect bites**. **Plant washes** treat **skin rashes and eczema**.

Use with caution as large amounts may cause toxicity; avoid during pregnancy or with blood-thinning medications.

Habitat and Description
From June through August, produces small, white, four-petaled flowers in airy clusters. Stems are square and grow 18–30 inches tall, with whorls of four narrow leaves marked by three veins. Thrives in **moist meadows, grasslands, and open forests**, spreading through **rhizomes** into **dense, fragrant colonies**.

Long-flowered Bluebells *(Mertensia longiflora)*

(Edible / Medicinal)

Traditional Uses and Cultural Significance

Long-flowered Bluebells grow in the rocky slopes and dry grasslands of our territory. While we don't carry extensive family knowledge of this particular species, we recognize it as part of the Mertensia family: plants known for their use as emergency greens.

The leaves and young shoots are edible, with a mouthfeel like other leafy greens and a mild grassy flavor. Best when young and lightly blanched or sautéed. The flowers are also edible and can be used as salad garnishes.

Used similarly to their relative species in traditional medicine, including respiratory support and topical applications for wound healing.

Health Benefits

Related Mertensia species have been used as **tea for nursing mothers** to increase milk flow. **Young leaves** provide **vitamins and minerals** when consumed as wild greens. Mild, flavor and mouth feel make them suitable for emergency food or spring salads.

Habitat and Description

Produces **bright blue,** tubular flowers that nod gracefully in dense, terminal clusters. Grows 5-25 cm tall from tuberous roots with few lance-shaped leaves. Blooms **April through June**.

Thrives in **dry grasslands, open forests, and rocky slopes**. **Drought tolerant** once established, preferring well-drained soils and full sun to light shade.

Comfrey *(Symphytum officinale)*

(Medicinal / Practical)

Traditional Uses and Cultural Significance

Comfrey has found its way into our practices through knowledge gathered from mentors, classes, family on both sides, and the willingness to do the work. Though not native to our territories, it has proven its medicine through use.

Known to our families as bone mend medicine. Science identifies the regenerative compound as allantoin.

We prepare poultices, ointments, and compresses for external injuries, knowing comfrey works powerfully with skin and bone. At the same time, we honor its boundaries: internal use is avoided due to the risks of liver toxicity from its alkaloids.

Comfrey also has a place in our ceremonial coffee substitutes. When roasted, the flavor deepens, taking on concentrated earthy tones similar to cocoa. Robust, yet mild enough to not taste like medicine. It blends well with other roasted plants and plants with ginger-like qualities, companions like roasted chicory, roasted dandelion, and *?ayut*. We don't drink it daily or excessively, but rather as a grounding, uplifting treat, something to ease ailments. Traditional or familial recipes are prepared through intention. Spirit, prayer, heart. Ceremony. As with most medicines, we practice moderation.

Health Benefits

External poultices, ointments, and compresses promote rapid healing of wounds, bruises, sprains, and bone fractures through cell-regenerating compounds like allantoin. Supports **musculoskeletal recovery** and **external tissue repair**.

Roasted roots and leaves occasionally blended in ceremonial coffee substitutes with other medicinal allies.

Internal use avoided due to liver toxicity risks.

Habitat and Description

Produces **drooping, bell-shaped flowers** in white to purple from May through August. Grows 30–150 cm tall with large, bristly leaves that extend down the stem.

A non-native species thriving in moist, fertile soils near settlements and disturbed areas.

ʔa·knuqɬuxunaʔtit mata, Wild Bergamot *(Monarda fistulosa)*

(Edible / Medicinal)

Traditional Uses and Cultural Significance
Wild Bergamot is one of our favorite plants to harvest. Our cache empties as soon as it's dried: we use it constantly in tea blends for daily wellness. The minty, oregano-like fragrance draws us to bergamot patches long before we see the distinctive purple flower clusters. We harvest the entire above-ground plant during flowering, bundling it to dry in our kitchen, where its scent fills the space with medicine. Our tea blends often feature bergamot as a base, combined with other seasonal plants to create warming drinks for colds, headaches, and digestive ease.

Its vigorous growth through spreading rhizomes means we can harvest frequently without depleting it. This abundance has made bergamot one of our teaching plants: we share it generously, showing others where they can harvest, gifting bundles to friends and elders. The confidence new learners gain through harvesting this plant runs deeper than technique. First smells drawing them in. First touch on a plant they're harvesting themselves. First taste from fresh-brewed tea made from what their own hands gathered. The depth of flavor often stirs memory. One elder, tasting fresh bergamot tea, was reminded of her mother making tea on the land. This is what we mean by experiential learning: knowledge that lives in the body, not just the mind.

Health Benefits
Leaves harvested before flowering offer different qualities than those gathered in bloom. Aromatic leaves contain **thymol and essential oils** with **strong antiseptic properties**.
Internal use: Warming tea treats colds, fevers, headaches, and digestive issues.
External use: Poultices for cuts and skin eruptions. Washes for sore eyes. Natural insect repellent.

Habitat and Description
Produces **pink-purple, tubular flowers** in dense clusters above leafy bracts from June through August. Grows 30-100 cm tall with square, aromatic stems and opposite, toothed leaves. Thrives in grasslands, meadows, and open forests.

Pink Wintergreen, Mata, *(Pyrola asarifolia)*

(Medicinal/Practical)

Traditional Uses and Cultural Significance

Pink Wintergreen grows quietly in the deep shade of coniferous forests, where we sometimes miss it during harvest. Knowledge carried through lineage and practiced hands-on in tea mixes.

Elders shared this knowledge with us, and they appreciate when we return the teachings to new learners. They especially appreciate when we treat them to the tea: it connects them to their familial stories and offers reprieve from their ailments.

The glossy, heart-shaped leaves remain evergreen, offering medicine year-round. Our knowledge holders have long used wintergreen for deep-seated pain and rheumatism.

We harvest carefully, respecting its slow growth and the mycorrhizal relationships with forest fungi it needs to thrive.

Health Benefits

Contains **methyl salicylate** for natural pain relief. Fresh leaf poultices treat wounds and bleeding. Root decoctions address liver complaints and kidney trouble. Leaf infusions serve as eyewash for inflammation. **Chewed leaves** offer rapid relief for pain. External applications preferred due to potency.

Habitat and Description

Produces **pale pink, nodding flowers** in elongated clusters of 10-25 blooms from June through August. Grows 10-47 cm tall with shiny, heart-shaped leaves in basal rosettes.

Thrives in acidic, humus-rich soils of closed-canopy coniferous forests. Forms colonies through creeping rhizomes from valley floors to subalpine zones. Requires mycorrhizal associations for establishment.

ɬawiyaɬ, Huckleberry (Vaccinium species)

(Edible / Medicinal / Spiritual / Practical)

Traditional Uses and Cultural Significance
Huckleberry is one of the first plants we introduced our daughter Ayla to, and most young learners if we are fortunate to be on the land when they are in season. *kȼiɬmitiɬq̓ɬikwaʔit* (August, fruit ripening during night) marks the time when families gather for harvest, their hands stained purple from picking for their kin.

This is a plant that didn't lose its place within common knowledge. As a little one, Ayla recognized grasshopper season as when the huckleberries are ripe, learning through observation.

We use the whole plant: dehydrated, fresh, preserved for jams, jellies, compotes, syrups, and teas for cold seasons. Huckleberry juice, frozen berries thawed and melted, is one of the best medicines in and of itself. Whether shared or a whole glass to gallon.

We have a specific cough medicine recipe gifted through time spent with Grandma Jenny during COVID-19. The elders who used it swore by it, and we continue to carry this gift forward.

Health Benefits
Berries are exceptionally high in **vitamin C, antioxidants, and anthocyanins**. Support cardiovascular health, immune function, and eye health. Leaf and berry teas serve as mild astringents for digestive issues and as anti-inflammatory remedies. Traditional use supports **blood sugar stabilization** and **respiratory health**.

Habitat and Description
Upright shrub reaching up to 2 meters tall. Produces sweet, **dark purple-black berries** from mid-summer into autumn. Serrate leaves. Small, urn-shaped flowers bloom before berries.

Thrives in mountain and forested areas from low to high elevations. A related species, nupxamuɬ (grouseberry), is a low-growing plant with red fruit that may be found growing with ɬawiyaɬ or on its own above treeline.

kwiɫqa ṱaʼqxaka, Common Burdock *(Arctium minus)*

(Edible / Medicinal / Practical)

Traditional Uses and Cultural Significance

Burdock has found a welcome home in our apothecary, despite its reputation as invasive. The plant is robust in shaded areas and resembles rhubarb in some ways.

Growing up we knew the plant through play as much as through medicine. The dry seed heads made great sticker projectiles, a handful of them causing laughter and sometimes difficulty removing them from one's, or a cousin's, hair.

This plant is used in our recipes for detox drinks, immune support, and coffee substitutes. We keep a spot open for the roots, which we dry and keep for later use in our teas and extracts. The young roots are edible raw or cooked, with a mildly sweet, earthy taste. We've also worked with the young leaves and stems, though older leaves require boiling in several changes of water to reduce bitterness.

Health Benefits

Roots are rich in **inulin** (supporting gut health), **vitamin C, potassium, and antioxidants**. Traditionally used as a blood purifier, diuretic, and anti-inflammatory medicine.

Poultices and salves from leaves or root treat bruises, burns, boils, acne, and skin conditions. Root and leaf teas support liver function, digestion, and chronic inflammation.

Use with caution for those with kidney issues due to high diuretic activity.

Habitat and Description

Biennial forming **large basal rosette of fuzzy leaves** in first year, sending up tall flower stalk (1–2 m) with purple, thistle-like flowers and sticky seed heads in second year. Spherical burrs cling to clothing and fur.

Thrives in **disturbed sites** like roadsides, riparian corridors, abandoned fields, forest edges. **Non-native species** that spreads aggressively.

Prairie Coneflower, Ratibida columnifera

(Medicinal / Spiritual / Practical)

Traditional Uses and Cultural Significance

This plant was taught by elders who valued plants with purging and cleansing properties. The root has been used as tea for colds and for internal cleansing.

The distinctive tall columnar cone surrounded by drooping yellow or reddish-brown petals makes this plant hard to miss in summer prairies. We observe it when we're on the land, watching the pollinators work the flowers, noting where it grows.

Elders taught that these teachings come through relationship and careful observation, not casual use. Plants with purging properties require knowledge and proper preparation.

Health Benefits

Root tea used for **colds** and as an **emetic for internal cleansing**. Related to other coneflowers that support immune function, though used with greater caution due to its purging properties. Traditional preparation requires knowledge and proper intention. External applications sometimes used for wounds.

Habitat and Description

Erect perennial growing **30–91 cm tall** with **deeply pinnate leaves**. **Distinctive flower** with **tall, columnar cone of purplish disk florets** surrounded by drooping yellow or reddish-brown ray petals.

Blooms **June through September**. Thrives in **dry, open, sunny places**: prairies, grasslands, hillsides, roadsides. **Drought-tolerant** once established. Excellent nectar plant for bees and butterflies.

ʔakinmiɬyukquɬaqpi·k, Labrador Tea *(Rhododendron columbianum)*

(Edible / Medicinal / Spiritual)

Traditional Uses and Cultural Significance

Trapper's tea is one we always have on hand, especially blended with *ʔayut* and huckleberry tea. Paired with our cough medicine, this gets us through the coldest winters.

When teaching Ayla about this plant, we had her smell it first, then look at the leaves closely. She found the bush herself and came back with a handful of the right plant. Then we had her taste it. Using our senses and being present is important to learning the language of the plants: we're training our palate, building recognition, trusting intuition, being present with our families and teachers, remembering our connection, preparing ourselves to carry knowledge.

An elder at one of our events tasted the tea and it brought her back to times on the land with her mother, drinking fresh steeped tea picked straight from the plant.

We harvest this the same time we pick *ʔayut*. The leaves have dusty orange coating on the underside: wait for this to fall off before harvesting. Deep green on top with silver underleaf. Can be mistaken for false azalea, though azalea leaves are more brittle once dried and more veiny.

Health Benefits

Tea from young leaves treats **respiratory complaints** (colds, cough, bronchitis), **fever, headaches, digestive issues**, and **mild pain**. Used topically as wash for burns, infections, skin rashes. Poultices for swelling and sprains. Insect repellent by bruising leaves and rubbing on skin.

Caution: Contains compounds that can be toxic if consumed in high quantity. Moderate use is standard practice.

Habitat and Description

Evergreen shrub, 0.5–2 m tall, spreading by rhizomes. Leaves deep green above, grayish below, edges rolled under; aromatic and sticky when crushed. White to cream, fragrant flowers in clusters (10–35), June–August.

Grows in **bogs, swamps, riparian areas**, and **wet forests** from **sea level up to 3,500 m**. Range: BC, Alberta, Montana, Washington, Oregon, Idaho.

naqpumsał, Fireweed (*Epilobium angustifolium*)

(Edible / Medicinal / Spiritual)

Traditional Uses and Cultural Significance

We've been to many fire sites where fireweed is abundant, observing the bumble and honeybees harvesting nectar from the bright magenta flowers.

We harvest this plant before the flower turns to fluff: cleaner that way. One of our fan favorite jellies is made from the flowers, fireweed jelly that never lasts long.

This plant is saved as green unfermented tea and black fermented tea, both giving different flavor profiles and properties. The black tea is particularly valued for men's and women's health: our cache empties as soon as it's ready, first come first served.

Young shoots, stalks, and leaves are edible: raw, cooked, or pickled. The inner pith is sweet and can be eaten fresh. Flowers are eaten fresh or used as colorful garnish.

Strong fibers from older stems used for twine, cords, and weaving. Fluffy seed down used as tinder or stuffing.

Health Benefits

Tea used for **soothing digestive tract issues, mild laxative, reducing inflammation**, and **calming skin irritations**. Poultices of leaves used for burns, wounds, boils, and skin rashes. Traditionally applied to ease bee stings, minor swelling, and sore throat.

Habitat and Description

Herbaceous perennial, 0.5–2 m tall; erect, reddish stems with alternate, narrow, lance-shaped leaves. Flowers are showy magenta to pink, four-petaled, in tapered terminal racemes. Seeds are small with silky hairs, wind-dispersed in late summer and fall.

Rapidly **colonizes burned and disturbed sites** like logged forests, avalanche slopes, open meadows, riparian areas, roadsides. Found from valley bottoms to subalpine and alpine zones. Can dominate the landscape a year or two after wildfire, stabilizing soils and providing pollinator habitat.

Important forage for bears, elk, porcupines, and beavers. Flowers pollinated by bumblebees, butterflies, and other insects.

Mata, Self Heal (*Prunella vulgaris*)

(Edible / Medicinal)

Traditional Uses and Cultural Significance

Self-heal is one of our favorite plants, one we've long known and worked with. The time and patience to harvest even an ounce of flowers requires dedication and integrity, remaining grounded in ʔa·knumuȼtitił.

We use the whole plant: flowers and leaves, in our tea blends, and we've experimented with the inflorescence in cakes, breads, and muffins. The flower holds its color well when dehydrated and cooked. The kids love knowing these treats were prepared with flowers, connecting them to the plants in a way that feels playful and delicious.

Our knowledge holders have long valued this plant. Tea or infusion supports general wellness, reduces fever, and eases mild digestive complaints. Applied as juice or poultice, it treats wounds, boils, and skin irritation. Young leaves make a good addition to salads raw or cooked as potherb: mild and nourishing.

Health Benefits

Antibacterial, anti-inflammatory, and **wound-healing** properties. Traditional use for sore throat, mouth sores, minor wounds, burns, diarrhea, stomach upset, and muscle pain. Mild astringent and antioxidant. Supports immune function.

Habitat and Description

Creeping perennial 6–20 inches (15–50 cm) tall, forming dense mats with square stems and oppositely paired leaves. Flowers are **compact spike of vibrant blue-purple florets**, blooming **June to October**.

Grows in **meadows, open woods, streambanks, roadsides, pastures, lawns**, and **moist to mesic soils** at elevations up to 2,500 m. Native to temperate regions; widespread in British Columbia and Montana.

Flowers visited by bumblebees, butterflies, long/short-tongued bees, and skippers. Forms dense mats beneficial to pollinator populations.

Mata, Anise Hyssop (*Agastache foeniculum*)

(Edible / Medicinal / Spiritual)

Traditional Uses and Cultural Significance

We have a love for all the mints. They come at different times of the year and all lend different depths of mint, used individually or together in tea blends.

This specific mint appears in our facial steams. We love how it enhances breathing, how it cools and calms the skin. We've done workshops where we offer tea tastings with take-home bundles, foot soaks, and facial steams with traditional plants.

Our knowledge holders, along with many Indigenous nations across the plains, have used anise hyssop for respiratory support: tea for coughs, colds, chest congestion, bronchitis. External poultices treat burns, wounds, and skin irritation. Tea relieves gas, bloating, mild diarrhea, and supports immune function. The smoke has been used to relieve depression and support emotional well-being.

Fresh leaves and flowers are eaten in salads, jellies, and baked goods. Seeds added to baked goods. Dried leaves for tea and potpourri.

Health Benefits

Tea serves as **expectorant, cough remedy, fever reducer**. Essential oils show **antiviral, antibacterial, and anti-inflammatory** properties. Rich in phenolic antioxidants. Supports lung, gut, and immune health. Carminative and aromatic—prevents and relieves digestive discomfort. Mildly sedative.

Habitat and Description

Aromatic perennial, **60–120 cm tall**, with **upright spikes of pale blue to purple flowers** and licorice- or anise-scented green leaves. Blooms midsummer to fall.

Native to northern U.S. Great Plains, British Columbia, and parts of Canada. Thrives in **prairies, open woodlands, and disturbed habitats. Drought-tolerant, deer-resistant**, grows in various soils.

Highly attractive to bumblebees, butterflies, and hummingbirds. Goldfinches feed on seeds after bloom.

Nasayit, Wood Lily (*Lily philadelphicum*)

(Edible / Medicinal / Spiritual)

Traditional Uses and Cultural Significance

We found this plant near Cranbrook within our traditional territory: bright orange in the middle of the forest, near a bog. The sight was captivating. Finding a plant so striking while we were building the idea of this book helped spark the vision forward.

Our familial teachers knew this as hard-times food, there when needed. Further research with other knowledge holders has shown: bulbs were cooked and applied to sores, bruises, swellings, and wounds. Medicinal tea made from the plant treats stomach problems, coughs, and fevers. Traditionally used to help women in labor deliver the afterbirth.

Health Benefits

Bulbs were also used as famine food: boiled, roasted, or dried when needed, though not a staple food source.

Ecological Notes

Nectar is important for **pollinators**, especially **butterflies and bees**. Lilies are sensitive to **livestock overgrazing**. More nature-minded, conservation-focused input should inform land management decisions in changing climate. Cattle pose real threats to traditional plant medicines and native ecosystems.

Habitat and Description

Herbaceous perennial, 0.5–1 m tall, unbranched stem with alternate leaves (sometimes whorled). Blooms June–August; orange to red (sometimes pink/yellow) upright flowers with six prominent tepals and purplish-brown spots at the yellow base.

Found in **prairies, meadows, open woods**, grassy balds, **moist forest openings**, and sometimes **disturbed habitats**. Prefers moderately moist to sandy, well-drained soils. Often pollinated by swallowtail butterflies and large day-flying moths.

niʔ¢na, Wild Carrot *(Daucus carota)*

(Edible / Medicinal / Practical)

Traditional Uses and Cultural Significance

This plant was shared by two early mentors. They said it was pretty rare. Over time, better harvesting areas were found, learning that while not uncommon, the small roots and scattered presence meant it was never a staple, just a supplement when encountered. The two knowledge holders were gracious teachers, trusting that learning would come through experience.

The mouthfeel was soft and not too mealy, maybe reminiscent of a boiled or older carrot. It was good out of the ground: soft at one point and woody/crisp in other parts. Though small, it was packed with flavor and carried similar flavor notes to garden carrots.

Wild carrot is an introduced plant (native to Eurasia, naturalized in BC and Montana), not a primary traditional food source, but recognized and used alongside native plants. Young roots are edible when tender: sweet, aromatic, but quickly become woody with age. **Leaves** can be used as herb, though may cause skin irritation when wet and exposed to sunlight.

Caution: Skin contact with foliage (especially when wet) may cause irritation. Seeds and older roots should be avoided unless properly identified, **many Apiaceae are toxic** and easily confused with wild carrot.

Health Benefits

Historically valued as diuretic, carminative, and mild stimulant. Used in teas for digestive support, to promote urination, and as remedy for kidney and bladder problems.

Habitat and Description

Biennial forming basal rosette in year one; in year two, produces hairy, branched stems (up to 1-4 ft tall) with feathery, carrot-scented leaves and distinctive flat-topped umbels of tiny white flowers, often with a purple central floret. Thrives in sandy, gravelly, well-drained soils, in full sun to partial shade. Found in fields, meadows, pastures, disturbed sites, roadsides. Supports bees, flies, small beetles, and diversity of pollinator species.

ʔakuwał, Wild Onion *(Allium cernuum)*

(Edible / Medicinal / Practical)

Traditional Uses and Cultural Significance

This woodland onion grows amongst the conifers from low to high elevation. All parts are edible: bulbs, leaves, flowers, with a mild sweet-garlic-onion flavor, similar in strength to cultivated onions.

The flowers can be dried and used for seasoning. They hold the flavor quite well. We use them in soups, stews, and other foods as a flavor enhancer. Our knowledge keepers have shared that onion and garlic were eaten to cleanse the system after long winters, adding both flavor and medicine to broths.

We like to eat them straight from the ground, whether chewing on the flower or eating the bulb. Good for dehydrating if you're building your apothecary.

Bulbs are roasted, boiled, or eaten raw. Leaves and flowers used in salads, for flavoring wild game, and as savory garnish.

Health Benefits

Traditional use for **digestive support and system cleansing**, particularly after long winters.

The **strong onion aroma** is key to safe identification. Carefully harvest when the plant is easily identifiable.

Habitat and Description

Herbaceous perennial, **20–60 cm tall. Slender bulbs** taper into **flat, grass-like, keeled leaves**.

Nodding, pink to pale-lavender bell-shaped flowers in loose, pendulous umbels 2–4 cm across, rising above foliage on arched, leafless stems. Blooms June–August. Characteristic onion smell and flavor.

Found in mixed conifer-hardwood forests, grassy open woods, dry meadows, rocky slopes, prairies, stream banks, from lowland valleys to montane habitats. Prefers full to partial sun and well-drained, moist soils. Forms colonies through bulbs and seeds.

Key nectar plant for **native bees, bumblebees, honey bees**, and pollinating insects. Generally avoided by mammalian herbivores.

ʔakukaʔɫak, Nine-leaf Biscuitroot *(Lomatium triternatum)*

(Edible / Medicinal / Practical)

Traditional Uses and Cultural Significance

This is one of our traditional food plants. One of our mentors talked about the food uses for this plant: it tastes better than the desert parsleys.

Elders recalled being able to pound and pulverize the roots (*ʔa·kukpukam*) into bricks that held well and had long shelf life. These worked both as portable food and as thickening agent.

Roots are eaten raw, roasted, or dried: high in carbohydrates, minerals, and dietary fiber. Used in ceremonial feasts and trade, sometimes ground and mixed with other tubers or berries for winter nutrition.

Health Benefits

Taproots and leaves prepared as teas for mild stomach upset, fever, or as spring tonic.

Habitat and Description

Herbaceous perennial, 20–60 cm tall, with deeply divided leaves forming 9 or more narrow segments. Umbels of small, bright yellow flowers produce clusters atop leafless stalks in spring. Flowers April–July.

Taprooted and drought-tolerant, resistant to competition from grasses and forbs. Adapted to moderately dry-to-moist soils, often on clay or rocky slopes, edges of forests, or grassland openings.

Found in grasslands, sagebrush steppe, meadows, and open or pine-dominated forests in valleys and montane slopes. Most common from foothills to lower montane elevations.

Flowers visited by **bees, flies, beetles**. Early season nectar source. Taproots help **stabilize soils** and support native biodiversity.

napknuququɫ, Desert Parsley *(Lomatium sp.)*

(Edible / Medicinal / Practical)

Traditional Uses and Cultural Significance

Knowledge of the Lomatium plants was shared by mentors on the land. Elders knew the varying species by different names, but for teaching purposes, they used terms like "biscuit root" to help learners understand the plant family.

This particular species was taught for more than just food: the dried, powdered root was used as foot powder. It kept footwear from developing odor and could be applied directly to the feet.

Young stems, taproots, leaves, and seeds have been used for nutrition and survival. Taproots are eaten raw, roasted, or dried, sometimes pounded and carried as travel food.

Used for coughs, colds, and as spring tonic. Lomatium dissectum is particularly notable for antiviral and antibacterial properties.

Health Benefits

Antiviral and antibacterial properties. Traditional use for respiratory support (coughs, colds). Spring tonic.

The foot powder use suggests antimicrobial and deodorizing properties.

Habitat and Description

Perennial, **aromatic herbs** with thick taproots and finely-divided "parsley-like" leaves. Umbel inflorescences bear yellow to creamy-white flowers (spring to early summer).

Adapted to dry, rocky soils, open grasslands, sagebrush ecosystems, and montane forests.

Early spring forage for deer, sheep, elk. Key host plant for pollinators and rare swallowtail butterflies.

ʔanaʔnam, Pineapple Weed (Matricaria discoidea)

(Edible / Medicinal)
Traditional Uses and Cultural Significance
This plant brings up childhood memories in our workshops. People remember finding it, popping the flower heads off, discovering it's edible. The stories are always about being a kid: curiosity, play, the satisfying pop of the little yellow cones.

We both learned in our early years that it's edible. If it wasn't being harvested, kids liked to pop the heads off. This plant, though small, grows in healthy colonies.

Flower heads and leaves are edible. Flowers are most often used for teas: a mild, fragrant herbal infusion with flavor reminiscent of pineapple and chamomile. They can also be eaten raw in salads (best before the plant begins to flower, as they turn bitter later). Some traditional berry mixes included pineapple weed flower heads as an aromatic.

The tea has calming effects.

Health Benefits
Traditionally used as mild sedative, digestive aid, antispasmodic, and anti-inflammatory. Tea or infusion taken for upset stomach, mild pain, colic, or as calming beverage before sleep.

External wash for sores and rashes.

Habitat and Description
Low-growing annual, strongly aromatic herb, 5–40 cm tall. Foliage is finely divided, feathery, and sweet-smelling. Flower heads conical, densely packed, greenish-yellow, lacking ray florets, and exude a strong pineapple-chamomile aroma when crushed.

Thrives in compacted, disturbed soils—footpaths, roadsides, waste-places, barnyards, pastures, driveways, garden edges, and playgrounds. Found wherever there is heavy human or animal traffic.

Native to northwestern North America and northeast Asia, now widespread across temperate northern hemisphere.

Attracts bees, beetles, flies, small butterflies—providing pollen and nectar in disturbed habitats. Very prolific and resistant to heavy human activity.

Curly-cup Gumweed, *(Grindelia squarrosa)*

(Edible / Medicinal)

Traditional Uses and Cultural Significance

This plant works well fresh from the stem: the resin stimulates saliva production, easing dry mouth on hot days. The resin has a mild minty quality.

We use it in teas and make cold and cough syrups from it: helpful for asthma, bronchitis, and coughs. It can be used as a makeshift or natural lozenge. Used externally for skin irritations and minor wounds.

We also use the resin and aerial parts in solar-infused oils, chest rubs, and ointments for insect bites and skin irritations.

Health Benefits

Anti-inflammatory, antimicrobial, and expectorant properties. Supports respiratory health. **External use** for skin irritations, insect bites, poison ivy.

Habitat and Description

Biennial or short-lived perennial, moderately branched with hairless, erect stems to 70 cm tall. Leaves are oblong to linear, with resinous or amber-tipped teeth, clasp the stem, and are often dotted with sticky glands.

Flowering heads are distinctive: yellow ray florets surround a large, resinous disk, and the green-tipped bracts strongly reflex (curl back). Blooms July–September in flat-topped clusters.

Thrives in disturbed areas, dry prairies, valleys, sagebrush steppes, and margins of wetlands or streambanks—especially where soils are sandy, gravelly, or moderately saline.

Fire- and drought-resistant, often thriving after disturbance or periods of dryness. Seeds dispersed by wind.

Pollinators include bumblebees, solitary bees, butterflies, and beetles. Important for pollinator support in prairie and disturbed-site succession.

ku¢uku, Pearly Everlasting
(Anaphalis margaritacea)

(Medicinal / Spiritual / Practical)

Traditional Uses and Cultural Significance

We use it in ceremonial tobacco blends. The smoke is calm, gentle.

In the sweat lodge, we place it on the rocks with other smudge plants to be inhaled as steam. When cold season brings coughs, especially for those with asthma or bronchial issues, the steam and smudging help.

We make tea blends and cough medicines with this plant. The tea works the same way as the steam.

The plant produces yellow dye for textiles.

Health Benefits

Traditional use for respiratory ailments (tea or smoke from aerial parts). Mild antiseptic and astringent for minor wounds, burns, and skin irritations. Used for headache relief.

Habitat and Description

Erect, rhizomatous perennial, 30–90 cm (1–3 ft) tall, with upright stems and clusters of small, pearly white flowers (papery bracts surrounding yellow centers) and narrow, silver-gray woolly foliage. Flowers bloom mid-summer to fall and persist long after blooming as dried heads.

Widely distributed across North America. Common in dry, sandy or gravelly soils, roadsides, meadows, prairie edges, sunny hillsides, and woodland openings from low elevations to subalpine.

Drought tolerant, thrives in nutrient-poor sites, adapts to disturbed and open landscapes. Spreads by underground rhizomes.

Important nectar source for bees and butterflies—especially the American Painted Lady butterfly (larval host plant). Deer resistant.

Chicory, *(Cichorium intybus)*

(Medicinal / Spiritual / Practical)

Traditional Uses and Cultural Significance

We use this in our seasonal coffee mixes. We also drink it as a cleansing tea when cutting back on caffeine or detoxing: helpful for liver support and digestion.

Roots are roasted and ground for a caffeine-free coffee substitute. They contain inulin, a prebiotic fiber that supports digestive health.

Young leaves can be eaten raw in salads. Older leaves are better cooked as greens: they get bitter when raw.

Health Benefits

Traditional use for liver support and digestive health. Mild laxative. Our elders have taught us about liver medicinal plants like this one, also used for skin complaints.

Caution: Excessive/prolonged use may cause sluggish digestion and vision issues. Milky latex can occasionally cause skin irritation.

Habitat and Description

Perennial or biennial herb, 30–120 cm (1–4 ft), exuding milky sap when broken. Leaves lobed and toothed; basal leaves forming a rosette; stem leaves clasp the stem.

Flowers are bright sky blue (rarely white or pink), 8–25 ray florets, about 2–2.5 cm across. Bloom July to early September.

Taprooted and drought-tolerant, often grows in rocky, hard-packed soils. Prefers disturbed soils—roadsides, fields, pastures, fencerows, and waste ground.

Native to Europe, widely naturalized across BC and Montana. Pollinators include various native bumblebees. Reproduces by seed; a single plant can produce up to 3,000 seeds each season.

skinkuȼ yaʔqitis, Wild Tarragon
(Artemisia dracunculus)

(Edible / Medicinal / Practical)
Traditional Uses and Cultural Significance
For cooking, we've learned to use it like other herbs. The scent and taste lean toward anise.

Flavor accompaniment for fish, game, and fowl. Can be used in stock and sauces. The ingredient lends itself well to savory style of cooking. Most wild herbs are milder than store plants which are bred for concentrated flavors.

The plant can be dried and stored as any herb. The scent imparts nicely in solar-infused oils for cooking and skincare.

Fresh leaves rubbed on hands or body work as an aromatic. Breathed through steam, it clears and calms.

Topical preparations of mashed or poulticed leaves have been used for insect bites and to reduce swelling.

Used as a ceremonial smudge, cleansing herb, and sometimes mixed into sweat lodge medicines or steams.

Health Benefits
Digestive support (soothe stomach, relieve flatulence). **Mild sedative and menstrual aid**. **External use** for insect bites and swelling.

Habitat and Description
Perennial, 2–4 feet tall with slender, linear to lance-shaped aromatic leaves. Clump-forming, spreads gradually by rhizomes. Produces small, greenish-yellow flowers in summer.

Thrives in dry, open meadows, prairies, roadsides, and disturbed habitats. Prefers full sun and well-drained soils. Drought-tolerant and deer-resistant, thriving in harsh, poor soils.

Goldenrod *(Solidago canadensis)*

(Medicinal / Spiritual / Practical)

Traditional Uses and Cultural Significance
We've learned this plant is a hair and scalp medicine. We use it as a steeped plant rinse or wash, or infused in solar oils.

We use the solar-infused oils specifically for sensitive skin formulas related to rosacea, eczema, acne, and acne scars.

Through learning from elders and through our own research and development, we've used infusions of leaves and flowers for sore throat, wounds, and urinary issues.

Health Benefits
Anti-inflammatory, antiseptic, and astringent properties. Supports **hair, scalp, and sensitive skin conditions**.

Habitat and Description
Tall perennial herb, typically 1–2.1 m (3–7 ft) with unbranched, erect stems, usually smooth but become fine-haired near the flower spikes.

Leaves are alternate, crowded along stem, lance-shaped, sharply toothed, mostly sessile (no stalk). Upper side smooth, lower side hairy, with prominent central vein and two lateral veins (triple-nerved).

Flower clusters are dense, elongated, arching, pyramid-shaped, with thousands of tiny yellow flowers. Each flower head has 10–17 yellow ray florets surrounding 2–8 yellow disk florets. Blooms July to October.

Thrives in moist to mesic soils, full sun to light shade. Common in meadows, roadsides, forest edges, prairies, ditches, and disturbed sites.

Spreads vigorously by both wind-dispersed seeds and underground rhizomes, forming dense colonies.

Very important for late-season pollinators: honey bees, native bees, butterflies, wasps, and beetles rely on it for nectar and pollen.

Elk Thistle *(Cirsium scariosum)*

(Edible / Medicinal / Practical)

Traditional Uses and Cultural Significance

This plant was taught as a seasonal treat. The young stalks are peeled and eaten: the mouthfeel is like celery crossed with cucumber, very succulent and crisp, with a snap.

It's one of the plants we've gotten to enjoy with our elders and knowledge keepers. One of the gifts of the land we got to experience together.

The tender, inner stalks and leaf bases are peeled and eaten raw or cooked. Harvesting is done early in the season when shoots are young.

Our elders shared stories in the mountains, remembering eating this plant straight from the ground. A little bit of salt and they had a snack that got them through their harvesting time. Joyous recollections of their childhood, younger years.

Health Benefits

Provides **dietary fiber, essential minerals** (calcium, potassium, iron), and **moisture**. The trek to high elevation to harvest this plant in early season—the fiber, minerals, and high moisture content made it valuable for hydration and energy, like eating an orange or drinking electrolytes after strenuous activity.

Habitat and Description

Native perennial with low, ground-hugging rosettes, deeply lobed and spiny leaves, and upright flowering stems that appear silvery due to dense hairs. Flower heads are pale lavender to white, solitary or few. Appears in meadows late spring to midsummer.

Thrives in moist to mesic soils, often at mid to high elevations in mountain meadows, subalpine grasslands, and forest clearings.

Valuable nectar and pollen source for native insects. Elk eat the flower heads early in the growing season. Songbirds, bees, and butterflies benefit from its blossoms. Taproot system helps stabilize sensitive soils.

Great Mullein, kipiɬkukakaʔmuɬ, (Verbascum thapsus)

(Medicinal / Spiritual / Practical)

Traditional Uses and Cultural Significance

Knowledge keepers have taught this plant as bone medicine: supporting central nervous system and mental health. We have learned that it is valued as bone and joint medicine, helps with skeletal and muscular ailments.

We use it in our traditional smoke mix. It is burned with other smudge and aromatics in the sweat.

Some knowledge holders use it as a tea. The plant needs to go through many washes before it is edible: it has fine hairs that need to be washed away.

Leaves are dried, de-haired, and smoked or brewed as tea for asthma, bronchitis, and chest infections. Flowers used for infusions to treat earaches.

Oils from leaves applied to wounds, rashes, and insect bites. The mucilage eases inflammation.

Health Benefits

Anti-inflammatory, expectorant, and demulcent properties. Contains mucilage, saponins, and tannins that ease inflammation and support respiratory function.

Habitat and Description

Tall biennial herb, up to 2 m tall. Rosette of large, soft, woolly basal leaves in year one, erect flower spike in year two. Long spike of small yellow flowers, blooming June to September.

Thrives in disturbed soils, roadsides, open meadows, and dry slopes, especially at lower elevations.

Introduced from Eurasia, now widespread across BC and Montana. Spreads by tiny seeds that remain viable for decades.

ʔa·kiʔɫmakʼ, Chokecherry *(Prunus virginiana)*

(Edible / Medicinal / Practical)

Traditional Uses and Cultural Significance

This plant brings warm memories: fires, roasting hot dogs and marshmallows on chokecherry sticks, telling stories and enjoying the change of seasons. Being present with loved ones.

This is an ingredient in the cough medicine we made with Grandma. We use it in our traditional food classes, showing historical use as chokecherry patties and in pemmican. Additionally, we share our newer recipes, like the cough syrup, the chokecherry syrup for pancakes and cheesecake, and even served with lime, mint, ice, tonic and sparkling water.

The bark is good medicine used for purging and cleansing after winter. The fruit is used fresh, dried, and often mashed for cakes, stews. Bark and root infusions used as traditional medicine for cough, colds, fevers, digestive complaints. The bark and twigs brewed for teas to calm sore throats, aid respiratory health, or for diarrhea. Flexible stems and wood used for tools, bows, arrows, and basket hoops.

Health Benefits

High in antioxidants, vitamins C, A, K, and several B-vitamins. Rich in dietary fiber. **Antioxidant and anti-inflammatory** properties support immune function and digestive health.

Seeds contain prussic acid: only fully ripe fruit should be used in quantity to minimize risk.

Habitat and Description

Shrub or small tree, 2–6 m tall. White flowers in hanging clusters, blooming May to June. Dark red to purple-black berries ripen July to September.

Thrives in moist areas, forest edges, stream banks, and open woodlands. Common across BC and Montana at various elevations.

Native to North America, widely distributed across our traditional territory.

Part Six: Fall
Walking Through Fall

"Hopefully, all families were able to gather and harvest everything they needed to get through summer. We usually know that we will have some extra: gifts for our elders and family members. We do this for those who cannot, for those who are remembering, and those yet to come."

As the wheel of the year turns toward ȼupnakutnamu, we feel the shift in our bones. Not just the cooling air or the changing light. Something deeper. A knowing that what we've been gathering all year is preparing us for what comes next.

Fall doesn't always announce itself with drama. Sometimes the change is so gentle you barely notice until one morning Ayla looks out the window and says, simply: "Fall is so beautiful!" The leaves have turned gold and red while we weren't looking. The white butterflies are already making their way home to the pines, dancing and gathering. September brings its swarms of stink bugs. Late afternoon air fills with webs when it's finally warm enough for spiders to fly. The bluejay returns in September or October, mimicking other birds. You look up expecting a hawk, only to hear the warble of a raven as the bluejay shows it's many talents before letting out its distinct screech.

Our daughter teaches us what we sometimes forget: every season has its own magic, its own lessons. Her excitement for Halloween reminds us that even as we prepare for winter's stillness, there's joy in the turning, beauty in the letting go.

Our kitchen comes to life: preparing and preserving. Jars line the kitchen island and labels need to be made. Some recipes are being born, others being tweaked, and others are remembered. Spirit guides during this time. Whether it is a scent, the sound of song, or hum. Spirit remembering spirit.

The memory of tûpye? (Grandma Jenny) feels especially close at this time of year. We move intuitively through the kitchen space: when to sweeten the mix, when to add more water, how much juice, how much pectin, how much love and spirit. Singing in our best hopes.

We prepare these medicines knowing the phone will ring. Someone's child with a cough that won't quit. An elder whose chest gets tight when cold settles in. Our own household needing something to ease a sore throat. We've learned from experience: winter asks for what we've gathered in fall.

And it's not just the physical harvest. Everything we've learned this

year about plants and protocols, about ourselves and what we're carrying. Fall is when we finally slow down enough to take stock.

The Invitation of Fall: Permission

We've been taught to ask for permission our whole lives.

We ask the plant before we harvest. We speak to Creator before we take. We honor our ancestors before we act. Permission is woven through everything we do. It's how we show respect, how we acknowledge we're part of something larger than ourselves.

But here's what we've learned: when was the last time you gave yourself permission?

Permission to feel what you feel without apologizing for it. Permission to release what no longer serves you. Permission to transform into something new. Permission to rest when your body asks for it. Permission to say no when your heart needs space. Permission to let go of thoughts that diminish you, even if you've carried them your whole life.

Fall isn't asking: did you gather enough to survive?

Fall is asking: are you ready to give yourself permission to transform?

Because here's the truth: **you are allowed. You've always been allowed.** Permission is aloud. Spoken, declared, claimed. You don't need to wait for someone else to give it to you. You don't need to earn it. You don't need to prove you deserve it.

You can give it to yourself right now.

Think about what you've done this year. If you've walked with us through spring and summer, you've been gathering. Plants and medicines, yes. Also teachings and protocols, stories and connections, memories and skills. You've been eating in ways that go beyond food. You've been nourished by the land, by teachers, by the work of your own hands, by relationships that sustain you.

And now fall asks you to stop.

Not because you're done. Not because you failed. Not because winter is coming to test you.

Transformation requires rest.

The caterpillar doesn't fear the cocoon. It doesn't brace for darkness. It simply knows: I've eaten. I've gathered what I need. Now it's time to stop moving, find a quiet place, and let something new emerge.

That's what fall prepares us for. Not survival through winter, but the deep rest that allows transformation. We're not defending against darkness. We're preparing to enter it intentionally, trusting that what feels like stillness is actually the most profound work we'll ever do.

Calling ourselves back

When we talk about "restoring spirit" or "calling ourselves back," we're not speaking in metaphors.

We tell our story through our actions. That's how others will interpret us, how our children will remember us, how the teachings will be carried forward. Not through what we say we believe. Through what we actually do.

How do we teach with humility when we've been called to teach?

How do we accept praise and gratitude when it's offered, without letting it inflate us or diminish us?

How do we give thanks for the gift of family, for belonging, for the long road we've walked through the seasons with the plants?

These aren't rhetorical questions. They're the actual work of fall. Checking our inventory not just of food and medicine, but of how we're showing up in the world.

Our spirit, our being, loves the natural world. We know this because we feel it. The way our whole body relaxes when we're on the land, the way our mind quiets when our hands are busy with real work, the way our heart opens when we share what we've gathered with someone who needs it.

And sometimes we have to call ourselves back. Back to presence when we've drifted into distraction. Back to focus when the work feels overwhelming. Back to feeling what we've learned instead of just knowing it intellectually. Back to remaining grounded when everything around us feels chaotic.

This is the practice of fall: calling ourselves back, again and again, so we can enter winter's transformation from a place of presence rather than escape.

Understanding What No Longer Serves

Here's what we've learned about self-actualization. We're not talking about some abstract philosophy that sounds good in theory but doesn't help you when you're standing in your kitchen at 2am wondering why you can't sleep, why your chest feels tight, why the same old patterns keep showing up no matter how hard you try.

Self-actualization is our ability to understand old thoughts and patterns and get rid of them when they no longer serve us.

That's it. That's the whole thing.

Here's what makes it hard: we have to be patient and vigilant with our minds when they try to diminish our hearts.

Your heart already knows where you're going. It knows what needs to happen, what wants to shift, what's ready to be released. Your brain, your thoughts, those are what put up the barriers. Your brain is the one saying: "But what if..." and "I can't because..." and "I've always been this way..." and "People like me don't get to..."

No more stinking thinking.

Fall is when we learn to recognize the difference between thoughts that serve us and thoughts that diminish us. And it's hard work, because some of those diminishing thoughts have been with us so long they feel like truth. They feel like protection. They feel like just "being realistic."

Old patterns don't disappear forever. They can show up even during times of happiness and joy. Especially during times of distraction. We think we've moved past something, and then one morning it's back, sitting in our chest like it never left.

This is not failure. This is the road strengthening us.

Challenges return. Hurdles reappear. People will test us. Old thoughts wait for us to stumble. They walk the same road we walk.

The difference is us. Each time we meet them, we're not the same person who stumbled before. We've grown. We've practiced. **We know the terrain now.**

We talked about this earlier: anger shows us where we need boundaries. Depression shows us where we need to learn from the past, not relive it. Anxiety shows us where we need vision. These teachers return. And each time, we have the chance to meet them from a stronger place.

Here's what we know: it's like grief, guilt, shame.

Name the thought. Name the emotion. Nurture it.

When you nurture something, when you actually acknowledge it, hold it with care instead of pushing it away, it knows it will be validated. It knows it's part of your experience, part of what you've survived, part of what shaped you.

It doesn't need to take all your attention.

It doesn't need to control your life.

It doesn't need to keep you from transforming.

We've walked this road before. We're stronger now.

We walked a painstaking road to get here. Years of carrying grief we wouldn't name, shame we wouldn't release, patterns we kept repeating because we didn't know we were allowed to stop.

We had to give ourselves permission.

Permission to love after loss. Permission to grieve without

apologizing for it. Permission to cry when crying was needed. Permission to breathe when our chests felt tight with everything we'd been carrying. Permission to transform without waiting for someone else to tell us we were allowed.

And here's what we discovered: this isn't new teaching. **This is blood memory.**

The ancestors already knew this. They practiced it. They lived it.

We're not teaching you something foreign. We're helping you remember what your body already knows.

Your body knows how to grieve. Your heart knows how to release. Your spirit knows how to transform. You've just been taught to ignore it, push it down, keep moving, stay productive, don't make waves, don't take up space, don't ask for what you need.

This is the teaching that brings people to tears in our workshops. Not because it's complex. Because the validation in the teaching finally gives them permission. Permission to feel without being consumed. Permission to release without feeling guilty. Permission to transform without waiting for someone else to tell them they're allowed.

It's the first time anyone's told them: You can feel it AND release it. You can honor it AND not be ruled by it. You can carry it AND still transform.

You are allowed to give yourself this permission.

Not because we're giving it to you. We can't. We're reminding you: you always had it. The ancestors left it in your blood. It's yours. It always was.

The Four Quadrants: Honest Inventory

Fall asks us to check our inventory across all four quadrants: physical, mental, emotional, spiritual. Not to judge ourselves, but to know ourselves. To see clearly what we have, what we need, what's working, what's not, what's ready to shift.

This is how we prepare for transformation. Not by pretending everything is fine. Not by white-knuckling our way through. By looking honestly at where we are and what we're carrying.

Physical: What Sustains the Body

The jars of preserved berries lined on cool shelves. The roots dried and bundled. The medicines prepared: cough syrup, immune tonics, salves for hands that work hard in cold weather. The firewood stacked. The skills practiced until they're second nature.

But also: is our body strong? Capable? Rested? Or are we running on fumes, ignoring pain, pushing through exhaustion because we

don't know how to stop?

Physical sovereignty means: your body is nourished and you know how to nourish it. You can care for yourself and your family. You're not dependent on systems that may or may not serve you. You stand on your own two feet.

Mental: What We Carry in Our Minds

The plant knowledge learned from teachers who were generous with their time. The processing skills that turn raw materials into medicine. The protocols remembered and followed. The seasonal timing observed year after year.

But also: what thoughts are we carrying that don't serve us anymore?

What beliefs about ourselves, about what's possible, about who we're allowed to be? What stories are we telling that keep us small?

Are we listening to our hearts, or are we letting our brains create barriers?

Fall is when we get honest about this. When we start to recognize: that thought right there, that belief I've carried for thirty years. That's not truth. That's trauma. That's what I learned to survive. And now it's become stinking thinking. I don't need it anymore.

Mental sovereignty means: your mind holds the knowledge you need AND you can challenge thoughts that diminish you. You can think clearly, plan ahead, remember what your teachers taught you. And you can release what no longer serves.

Emotional: What We Haven't Processed

The grief of this year. What was lost, what didn't grow, who we miss. The regulation we've practiced (or haven't). The presence we've cultivated with our children, our partners, our community. The ways we've numbed or avoided when things got hard.

Fall slows us down enough to feel what we've been carrying.

Spring and summer keep us busy. There's always something to harvest, preserve, teach. Fall says: stop. Sit down. Feel this.

Are we present with our families, or are we performing presence while our minds are somewhere else?

Are we using substances: alcohol, weed, sugar, screens, to manage emotions we don't want to feel?

Can we sit with grief without being destroyed by it? Can we feel shame without letting it define us? Can we hold guilt without letting it control us?

Name it. Nurture it. Validate it. This is the practice. Not pushing emotions away. Not letting them consume us. Holding them with care while knowing they don't get to take all our attention.

Emotional sovereignty means: you can feel what you feel without being destroyed by it. You can regulate yourself. You're present. Not perfect, but honest. And you're ready to transform.

Spiritual: How We Walk in the Web

The protocols we've followed. The gratitude we've practiced. Not just in words, but in actual action. The offerings we've made. The prayers spoken before harvest, during processing, when sharing with others.

But also: do we know our place in the web, or are we still trying to live above it?

How do we teach with humility when people tell us we've changed their lives?

How do we accept praise and gratitude without letting it make us think we're special?

How do we give thanks for family and belonging when we know how many people don't have that?

Spiritual sovereignty means: you know your protocols. You understand your responsibilities. You're connected to the web. Ancestors behind you, descendants ahead of you, land beneath you, community around you. You're not alone. You never were.

And you know that teaching, healing, helping: none of that makes you better than anyone else. It just means you've been given something to share. And sharing it with humility is how you honor the gift.

Mapping What's Ready to Shift

This is the practice of fall: sitting with what we've gathered (physically, mentally, emotionally, spiritually) and asking honestly:

What's working? What's not? What's ready to change?

Not someday. Not when circumstances are perfect. Not when we feel ready.

Now. What wants to shift now?

Spring taught us: timing matters. Some things can't be rushed.

Summer taught us: abundance comes from consistent work, from showing up even when it's hot and hard.

Fall teaches us: letting go is part of the cycle. Release is how we make room for what's next.

And sometimes what we need to release isn't a thing. It's a thought. A belief. A story we've been telling about who we are, what we're capable of, what we deserve.

Your heart already knows what needs to be released. Your brain is the one arguing for why you need to keep holding on.

Fall asks: are you ready to listen to your heart?

Those Who Cannot, Those Remembering, Those Yet to Come

We don't do this work just for ourselves.

Those who cannot: Elders who can no longer gather. Community members struggling with illness, injury, grief. Families just learning to return to these practices. Do we have enough to share? Are we teaching what we know?

Those remembering: People reclaiming knowledge after generations of disconnection. Urban Indians finding their way back. Youth discovering what their grandparents knew but couldn't pass on. Anyone who's been cut off from territory, from language, from protocols. Are we creating pathways for them to learn? Are we holding space for their return?

Those yet to come: Children and grandchildren who will need this knowledge when the world shifts. Who will need to know how to feed themselves from the land, how to make medicine, how to recognize when thoughts don't serve them, how to name and nurture emotions, how to transform. Are we preserving this? Are we passing it forward?

This is why everything we do matters. Not because we're special. Not because we have it all figured out. Because we're part of a web that extends beyond us in all directions. Past, present, future.

What we gather, we share. What we learn, we teach. What we transform in ourselves creates possibility for others to transform too.

The Practice of Calling Ourselves Back

"Each footprint we leave connects us to the past, grounds us in the present, and guides us to the future. We learn to tread lightly and pace ourselves through mindfulness, intention, and prayer."

This is how we prepare for winter's transformation:

Mindfulness: Paying attention to what actually is. Not what we wish it was, not what it should be, but what it is. The state of our pantry AND the state of our hearts. The medicines we've prepared AND the thoughts we're carrying. The food we've preserved AND the emotions we've been avoiding.

What's true right now? What's actually happening?

Intention: Based on what we notice, what needs attention? If we're running low on cough syrup, we make more. If we're emotionally reactive with our kids, we work on regulation. If our brain is creating barriers, we practice listening to our hearts. Intention turns awareness into action.

Prayer: Not just words. The entire practice of engaging with the web. Asking, receiving, giving thanks, honoring, sharing. Prayer is what connects everything. It's how we acknowledge: we're not doing this alone. We're held by ancestors, guided by teachers, supported by land, connected to community.

Prayer is what prepares us to enter winter's cocoon with trust instead of fear.

Gathering Between Seasons

For those who cannot. For those just remembering. For those yet to come.

By late autumn, we move with quieter hands. The bright, urgent work of summer gives way to steadier rhythms. Picking what remains after frost, digging where the earth still loosens, listening for what the land offers when we're finally still enough to hear.

This physical work grounds everything else we've been talking about. While we're reflecting on thoughts and emotions, our hands stay busy. Mind and body, heart and hands, all working together.

We store what we can. Glass jars on cool shelves. Bundles hung where air moves. Salves cured in quiet corners. We label with season and place. We tell the story of the day we gathered, who helped, what was remembered.

Nothing here is spare. Everything has a task.

This is reciprocity the land teaches. Fall asks us to gather wisely and prepare. Winter asks us to sit with what we have, to rest, to transform. We keep our protocols close: harvest with clean tools, take modestly, choose healthy stands, protect roots and water, give thanks in form and action.

The promise we make now is the promise that green endures under snow. Waiting, like us, to emerge.

Autumn Equinox: The Balance Point

Prayer of Gratitude, Keepers of the Seasons

Creator, we thank You for the harvest, for the fruits of our labor and the labor of all creation. We give thanks for the hands that gathered, for the roots that held, for the rains that nourished.

As we stand between light and shadow, between receiving and giving, between speaking and listening, between holding and releasing, we ask that You walk with us gently now.

Make us aware of the beauty of endings and the promise of renewal. We offer gratitude for the cycle that sustains us, for the medicines that will carry us through seasons ahead, for the transformation that awaits us in winter's cocoon.

Reflection: The Medicine of Gratitude

Autumn teaches us the medicine of gratitude. Giving thanks is not an end. It is a beginning.

We gave ourselves permission. To feel without apologizing. To release what no longer serves. To transform without waiting for someone else to allow it.

We called ourselves back. Again and again. Back to presence, back to focus, back to feeling what we've learned instead of just knowing it.

We named the thoughts that diminish us. We named the emotions we've been carrying. We nurtured them. We validated them. And we learned they don't have to control us.

We checked our inventory. Physical, mental, emotional, spiritual. Not to judge ourselves. To know ourselves.

We remembered: we don't do this work alone. Those who cannot. Those just remembering. Those yet to come. We gather for all of them.

And now, gratitude.

In this balance between abundance and stillness, we honor the hands that helped us gather, the hearts that taught us to share, the land that never stopped giving.

Every offering we make now: a jar of jam, a bundle of herbs, a whispered prayer, a challenged thought, a named emotion, a released pattern. Each one is a seed for next season's growth.

The caterpillar teaches us that entering the cocoon is not ending. It is transformation. What feels like stillness is actually the most profound work we'll ever do.

As the air cools and light fades, we bow to the earth and whisper:

Thank you, thank you, thank you.

Everything Connects

You are not alone in the cocoon. You are held. By ancestors who walked this path, by land that supports every step, by teachers who shared what they knew, by family and community.

You're not transforming because you're broken. You're transforming because that's what living things do. Seeds become plants. Caterpillars become butterflies. Children become adults. Grief becomes wisdom. Pain becomes medicine.

Your heart already knows.

Winter gives you time to listen. Time to be still. Time to rest so deeply that when spring comes, when you emerge, you'll be something new.

Not because you were never good enough. Because you were always meant to become more than what you started as.

When we walk through the seasons, when we gather with respect, when we challenge thoughts that don't serve us, when we name and nurture emotions, when we listen to our hearts, we're practicing permission.

Permission to be in right relationship. With the land. With each other. With ourselves.

This is returning to self and land.

This is restoring spirit.

This is calling ourselves back.

Summer nourishes us. Fall prepares us. Winter holds us. Spring emerges us.

q̓anɬat̓ana, Whitebark Pine *(Pinus Albicaulis)*

(Edible / Medicinal / Spiritual)

Traditional Uses and Cultural Significance

Whitebark pine grows in subalpine and alpine zones where most trees cannot survive. Industry just about wiped them out. Limber and Whitebark were seen as being in the way and not useful. Blister rust and beetle kill finished what logging started. Even through conservation and repopulation efforts, they remain a threatened species.

We harvested the seeds (pine nuts) for high-energy food long before the tree became endangered. Roasted, raw, or ground into meal. People knew where the trees grew, when cones ripened, how to harvest what was needed.

We use the needles for tea. Respiratory support and immune strength. The resin becomes salve for wound care and chest rubs. During COVID, whitebark pine became essential medicine, part of what we now call Ka Papa teachings: what our grandfather knew combined with what the tree offered. Medicine that helped our elders breathe when hospitals were overwhelmed.

The seeds are nutrient-dense when ethically gathered. We rarely take them. Wildlife depends on them more than we do.

Health Benefits

Pine needle tea: Vitamin C, antioxidants. Supports respiratory function and immune system.

Resin: Antimicrobial, anti-inflammatory. Used in salves for wounds, skin irritation, chest congestion.

Seeds: High in healthy fats, protein, vitamins, minerals. Sustaining food when gathered with permission and in balance.

Habitat and Description

Long-lived conifer, 20-25 meters tall or wind-sculpted into low krummholz at timberline. Yellow-green needles in bundles of five. Thin whitish-gray bark, gnarled with age. **Short purple cones that require fire or animals to release seeds.** Range: Subalpine zones, British Columbia to Montana, northern Rockies, Pacific Northwest.

Keystone species that holds soil, shades snowpack, feeds bears and birds. Threatened by white pine blister rust, mountain pine beetle, climate change.

ʔakuk'pɬuɬaɬ, Rocky Mountain Juniper (*Juniperus scopulorum*)

(Edible / Medicinal / Spiritual)

Traditional Uses and Cultural Significance

Juniper might be the first smudge we ever remember using. In ceremony, steeped for tea, added to cleansing baths. It's been with us from the beginning. Over the years, we've had the privilege of bringing people onto the land to teach what we know, keeping traditional knowledge alive through hands-on learning.

In sweat ceremonies, we often blend juniper with other smudge plants. We also teach salve-making. Traditional preparations that carry these sacred plants into everyday wellness. Someone once shared how our juniper salve recipe became part of their own healing, and how they've since passed that knowledge forward. That's exactly how it's supposed to work. Hand to hand, person to person, the teachings spreading through relationship.

We have long used juniper as medicine. Teas or infusions made from berries or young sprigs support kidney and urinary health, ease digestive complaints, and help with respiratory issues. Berries were sometimes chewed, boiled, or roasted for their distinctive flavor.

Health Benefits

Juniper works across body and spirit. **Teas from berries or sprigs** act as diuretic, supporting kidney and urinary tract health, easing digestive complaints and respiratory issues. The smoke carries ceremonial power for purification and protection. **In salves, juniper brings antimicrobial properties, traditionally used for joint pain and skin support.** Berries add piney depth to wild game and are essential in gin-making.

Habitat and Description

Small to medium evergreen, 6-15 m tall, narrow pyramidal crown. Slow-growing. Reddish-brown bark sheds in strips. Scale-like bluish-green leaves pressed to branches. Berry-like cones that are waxy blue or bluish-purple, 6-8 mm, ripen September-October, 1-3 seeds per cone.

Dry ridges, rocky slopes, open woodlands, foothills to mid-elevations (7,500 ft). British Columbia, Alberta, Montana, Rocky Mountains. Survives drought, wind, fire. Holds soil, provides winter food and shelter for birds and mammals.

ʔiȼhat, Western Red Cedar (Thuja plicata)

(Medicinal / Spiritual / Practical)

Traditional Uses and Cultural Significance
We've been privileged to walk the old growth sections of our territory, visiting ancient cedars and hemlocks. Trees the were well over 300 years old. **Cedar shows up in nearly every part of life: smudge, trade, tea, medicine.**

We use it in tea blends, foot soaks, medicine steams, sweat ceremonies, and traditional salves. We've also taught with the bark, showing people how to make cedar spoons, bowls, baskets, and even miniature baskets for earrings.

Cedar is the Tree of Life. The cornerstone of culture, spirituality, survival. The wood built dugout canoes from single massive trunks. Roots became cordage for baskets and binding bark to canoe frames. Bark and roots woven into baskets, mats, rope, regalia. Branches burned for smudging, placed in sweat lodges for purification and protection.

Health Benefits
Cedar leaf and bark infusions support respiratory health, ease joint pain, and help with colds and coughs. Steam from cedar opens airways and clears congestion. Topical use (in baths or salves) provides pain relief and antimicrobial support.

Habitat and Description
Massive, long-lived evergreen, reaching over 60 m tall and 7 m diameter, often buttressed at base. Red-brown or gray-brown fibrous bark peels in long strips. Aromatic, glossy, scale-like leaves arranged in flat sprays. Small woody seed cones (10-12 mm) ripen mid-summer to fall.

Moist forests of Pacific Northwest, British Columbia (including Ktunaxa territory), western Montana, Idaho, northern California, Alaska. Thrives in low-elevation wet forests with abundant rainfall. Provides shelter for birds, mammals, and ecosystem protection. Deer, elk, and black bears feed on seedlings, bark, and sapwood.

ʔaquɬaqpi·s, Creeping Dogbane
(Apocynum cannabinum)

(Practical / Medicinal)

Traditional Uses and Cultural Significance

We use both creeping dogbane and the larger spreading variety for Indian hemp. Strong fiber for cordage. Both grow abundantly throughout our territories.

This is often one of our winter projects at home or in workshops. An introduction to traditional knowledge and skills, hands-on experience with what the land offers. Processing dogbane teaches patience, respect for timing, and the importance of knowing when to harvest. The plant shouldn't be picked while it's still green and the sap is running.

Even when dried and harvested at the right time, dogbane can have a numbing effect on the body. Fine slivers work their way into skin during processing, and the plant's compounds affect circulation and sensation. This isn't dangerous in small amounts, but it teaches you to work carefully, respect what you're handling.

We have valued ʔaquɬaqpi·s for its fibrous stems. Harvested late summer or early autumn, fibers were extracted by soaking, pounding, and twisting stems into cordage strong enough for fishing nets, bowstrings, snares, thread, fish traps, snowshoes, and other survival needs.

Health Benefits

Dogbane is primarily a **material plant, not medicinal** for most purposes. The cardiac glycosides it contains are potent and toxic. **Not for casual use.** Specialized knowledge holders in some traditions used it for heart-related conditions, but this requires deep understanding of dosage and preparation.

Habitat and Description

Perennial herb, 30-120 cm tall. Red-tinged stems, spreading or erect. Opposite, elliptical to lance-shaped leaves with distinctive milky sap. Small bell-shaped white or pink flowers in clusters at stem tips, blooming June-August. Slender paired seed pods with silky-haired seeds.

Thrives in sandy, gravelly, or moist soils. Open woods, stream banks, meadows, disturbed sites. Deep roots stabilize soil. Distributed across North America, extensive populations in British Columbia and Montana.**All parts toxic to livestock and humans.**

naɬi·ćaxawuʔk, Devil's Club (*Oplopanax horridus*)

(Edible / Medicinal / Spiritual / Practical)

Traditional Uses and Cultural Significance

We set out to know and have relationships with as many plants as we can. We especially enjoy the plant community. The stories they share, what they've heard from teachers or the plants themselves, even dreams and firsthand experiences with plants we may not know yet.

Devil's club has an intimidating name. It's one of the kindest plants we've met. Not approaching it mindfully may end in a quick lesson about treading lightly. The plant shares its medicine generously as tea, cambium to eat, and bark for smudge.

The roots are not as protected as the rest of the plant. Best practice is to work from the root up when harvesting. There are usually two harvest times. Early spring or later in fall, when the plant's energy is either rising or settling.

The scent is inviting, beautiful. Once you know it, it stays with you. The cambium is a delicious treat, like a lozenge. We burn it powdered in the sweat, use it similar to smudge, infuse oils for medicine. Dry, powder, and drink as tea.

Health Benefits

Root and bark infusions treat rheumatism, arthritis, joint pain, tuberculosis, diabetes, colds, cough, and digestive complaints. Antibacterial, hypoglycemic, anti-inflammatory. Supports kidney and metabolic health. Topically, salves and poultices treat wounds, infections, inflammation, and skin conditions. The cambium can be chewed for respiratory health and immune strength. Spiritually, it clears negative energy, sets boundaries, helps ceremonial work.

Habitat and Description

Shrub, 1-3 meters tall (up to 5 meters in undisturbed areas). **Large palmate leaves (20-40 cm across) with 5-13 lobes, sharply toothed, covered in yellow brittle spines on both surfaces and veins. Woody stems densely armed with irritating spines.** Robust spreading roots form clonal colonies via rhizomes.

Tiny greenish-white flowers in dense pyramidal clusters at stem tips, spring to early summer. Bright red berries (drupes) in late summer. **Moist, shaded habitats throughout** British Columbia, Montana, and Idaho.

ʔayut, Bear Root (*Ligusticum porteri*)

(Edible / Medicinal / Spiritual / Practical)

Traditional Uses and Cultural Significance

Bear root holds some of our best mountain memories. Harvesting with our family, learning to identify the mane or whiskers (key markers for new learners), taking time and patience to get the whole root out of rocky ground. This plant requires intention. Hands-on experience is the best teacher.

We love gifting bear root to elders and sharing it at workshops. We've made cough syrup, cough drops, infused honey, and solar-infused oil from it. The plant is versatile. Great straight from the ground, or as a chunk bitten from the dry root for immediate relief.

Bear root is culturally valued, which makes it susceptible to commercial and disrespectful harvesting. Sustainable harvesting and respect for territory matter.

We chose bear root because it's closer to us for harvesting. The plant varieties we teach about and use are closely related. We use Bear Root and Osha Root interchangeably to protect integrity within specific regions.

We use ʔayut for respiratory ailments. Coughs, colds, bronchitis, sore throat. Prepared in teas or decoctions. It also supports digestive health, pain relief, and immune strength with antimicrobial and antiviral effects.

Health Benefits

Bear root is a **powerful** respiratory medicine. Expectorant, anti-inflammatory, clears mucus, soothes sore throat. The root's warming and stimulating properties improve respiratory function. Can be chewed fresh or dried for immediate relief, prepared in teas, tinctures, cough syrups, or infused in honey and oils.

Habitat and Description

Perennial herb, 50-100 cm tall, fern-like deeply divided leaves. Thick, woody, aromatic taproot with strong celery-like or licorice scent. **The "mane" or root whiskers are key identifiers.** White flowers in flat-topped umbels, late summer. Reddish, ribbed, oblong fruits. Moist, shaded environments: stream banks, forest understories, moderate to high elevations. British Columbia, Montana, western North America. **Slow-growing, so it requires sustainable harvesting to preserve wild populations.**

Evergreen Needles, ʔa·kuɫaɫ and Tree Resin, ʔiɫwas

(Edible / Medicinal / Spiritual / Practical)

Traditional Uses
We gather tree needles and tips during spring and fall. They're one of the most abundant teas and medicines available. Balsam fir makes beautiful infused oil and is used for smudge and aromatic purposes. Many of these teas, steams, and smudges support grounding, grief and emotional work, personal and spiritual ceremony. Always available, easy to gather, versatile in use.

Needle infusions were steam-inhaled or added to sweat lodge ceremonies for respiratory cleansing. Bundles of aromatic needles served as bedding, deodorizer, and spiritual purifiers.

Sap and resins are good for wounds, practical use, toothaches, fire starters, waterproofing baskets and canoes. Infused in oils, used sparingly as thickening agent in salves. Pine, spruce, and fir resins work as topical antiseptics for cuts, burns, boils, infections, and skin irritations.

Resin was chewed as natural gum. Fresh for dental care, dried as breath freshener. **Used in ceremonial fires and smudges.**

Health Benefits
Evergreen needle teas provide Vitamin C, respiratory support, immune strength. Steam inhalation clears congestion, supports lung health. **Resins** are antimicrobial, antiseptic when applied topically for wound care, dental health, skin irritations. Small internal doses (carefully prepared) treat coughs, digestive issues, act as mild expectorant.

Habitat and Description
Evergreen conifers (pine, spruce, fir, balsam fir) grow throughout British Columbia, Montana, and western North America. Found from low valleys to high elevations. Needles vary by species. Pine in bundles of 2-5, spruce and fir needles single, attached directly to branches.

Resin (pitch/sap) appears where bark is damaged or cut. Fresh resin is sticky, aromatic. Dried resin hardens, can be chewed or powdered. Spring tips are soft, light green, best for tea. Fall needles are mature, still potent for infusions.

The Medicine Begins: Teas, Tonics, & Elixirs of the Seasons

We've walked through the seasons, learned to gather with permission and reciprocity. Now the medicine begins when we slow down enough to notice. Not rushing through preparation, but being present with the plants as they transform from leaf and root into tea, tonic, elixir.

What follows is knowledge that lives in blood memory, carried forward through generations of hands making medicine. When you make these teas and tonics, you join a lineage of people who understood that medicine isn't something we buy, but something we make with our own hands from what the land provides. **This is the pause between gathering and winter's rest. A time to transform abundance into sustenance.**

Start with what grows where you live. Trust your hands. The plants will guide the rest.

Teas & Infusions

Spring Cleansing Tea

Ingredients

- Nettle leaf
- Violet flower
- Dandelion leaf and root
- Chickweed
- Optional: slice of lemon or touch of honey

Instructions

- Combine equal parts of each herb. Use 1–2 teaspoons per cup of hot water.
- Steep covered for 10 minutes.
- Drink 1–2 cups daily for two weeks in early spring.

Properties: Cleansing, detoxifying, mineral rich.

Taste: Bitter-sweet, green, earthy, lightly floral.

Energetics: Cooling, drying.

Uses: Supports liver and kidney function, clears winter stagnation, restores vitality after illness, and rejuvenates the body as spring arrives.

Summer Cooling Tea

Ingredients

- Wild rose petals
- Mint
- Fireweed blossom
- Pineapple weed

Instructions

- Infuse herbs in sunlight for 4–6 hours in clear glass.
- Chill and enjoy cold or at room temperature.

Properties: Cooling, uplifting, digestive, mildly astringent.

Taste: Floral, minty, slightly sweet, and bright.

Energetics: Cooling, moistening.

Uses: Soothes heat and irritability, refreshes the body after work or a day in the sun.

Heart of Summer Elixir Tea

A tea for the emotional heart

Ingredients

- Fresh rose petals
- Wild strawberries
- Small handful of hawthorn leaves and flowers
- Honey to taste

Instructions

- Mash berries and petals together.
- Pour warm (not hot) water over them.
- Let steep 20 minutes.
- Strain and sweeten gently.

Properties: Cardiotonic, nourishing, mood-elevating.

Taste: Sweet, floral, slightly tangy.

Energetics: Warming, moistening.

Uses: Strengthens the emotional heart, eases grief, and restores gentle joy and balance.

Autumn Immune Support Tea
Ingredients
- Elderberries
- Yarrow
- Goldenrod
- Burdock root

Instructions
- Simmer 1 tablespoon of berries and roots for 20 minutes.
- Add flowers in the last 5 minutes.
- Sweeten with honey if desired.

Properties: Antiviral, immune-supportive, lymphatic stimulant.

Taste: Earthy, floral, mildly bitter, grounding.

Energetics: Warming, drying.

Uses: Supports immune resilience, clears congestion, and prepares the body for colder seasons.

Winter Warming Tea
Ingredients
- Douglas-fir tips
- Rosehips
- Osha root
- Spruce tips

Instructions
- Simmer gently for 15–20 minutes.
- Sweeten with honey or maple syrup.

Properties: Respiratory-supportive, immune-building, comforting.

Taste: Resinous, tart, and softly spiced.

Energetics: Warming, moistening.

Uses: Encourages deep breathing, supports the immune system, and connects one to rest.

Elderberry & Cedar Cough Brew
Ingredients
- Elderberries
- Cedar needles (small pinch)
- Wild ginger root
- Honey

Instructions
- Simmer berries and ginger for 15 minutes.
- Add cedar in the final minute, then strain.
- Sweeten with honey.

Properties: Antiviral, expectorant, respiratory tonic.

Taste: Warming, spicy, resinous, sweet.

Energetics: Warming, drying.

Uses: Eases chest congestion, promotes expectoration, opens breathing passages, and centers the spirit in gratitude.

Juniper Digestive Tea
Ingredients
- 1 teaspoon crushed juniper berries
- 1 cup hot (not boiling) water
- Optional: touch of honey or mint

Instructions
- Lightly crush the juniper berries to release their aroma.
- Pour hot water over them and steep, covered, for 5–7 minutes.
- Strain and sip slowly with gratitude.

Properties: Digestive, antiseptic, detoxifying.

Taste: Piney, resinous, slightly bitter with a lingering sweetness.

Energetics: Warming, drying.

Uses: Supports digestion, eases bloating, clears stagnation, and helps calm the nerves.

HIGH MOUNTAIN LUNG SUPPORT TEA
Ingredients
- 1 teaspoon Labrador tea (High Mountain tea)
- 1 teaspoon wild mint
- 1 teaspoon willow bark
- A few rosehips or spruce tips (optional for vitamin C and balance)

Instructions
- Combine herbs and pour over 2 cups of hot water.
- Steep covered for 10–15 minutes.
- Strain and serve warm.

Properties: Respiratory tonic, expectorant, antimicrobial, antioxidant.

Taste: Resinous, herbal, slightly sweet with a cooling finish.

Energetics: Cooling, drying.

Uses: Supports lung function and recovery after colds or smoke exposure.

WATER INFUSIONS

SPRING RENEWAL WATER
Ingredients
- Fresh pine tips or spruce tips
- Lemon slices
- Handful of wild mint leaves
- Cold spring or filtered water

Instructions
- Lightly bruise herbs and citrus, then submerge in a glass jar of water.
- Let infuse in sunlight for 1–3 hours.
- Strain and refrigerate.

Properties: Cleansing, energizing, mineral rich.

Taste: Bright, resinous, citrusy.

Energetics: Cooling, drying.

Uses: Clears mental fog, awakens the body, and supports gentle detoxification.

Summer Berry & Wildflower Water
Ingredients
- Fresh strawberries, raspberries, or serviceberries
- A few wild rose petals
- Slice of cucumber
- Cold water

Instructions
- Combine ingredients in a pitcher.
- Infuse for 2–4 hours in the refrigerator.
- Strain and serve cold.

Properties: Hydrating, antioxidant, anti-inflammatory.

Taste: Sweet floral with soft fruit tones.

Energetics: Cooling, moistening.

Uses: Replenishes electrolytes and calms digestion.

Winter Evergreen & Citrus Infusion
Ingredients
- Sprig of Douglas-fir or cedar
- Slice of orange or grapefruit peel
- Touch of honey (optional)
- Warm water (not boiling)

Instructions
- Pour warm water over ingredients and steep for 10 minutes.
- Strain before drinking.

Properties: Immune-supportive, uplifting, gently expectorant.

Taste: Resinous, bright, lightly sweet.

Energetics: Warming, moistening.

Uses: Refreshes indoor airways and lifts the mood.

TONICS & ELIXIRS

Morning Greetings Tonic
A tonic for renewal and courage

Ingredients

- ½ cup violet flowers
- ½ cup dandelion blossoms
- ½ cup fresh cleavers
- Raw honey to cover

Instructions

- Place all herbs in a clean glass jar.
- Pour honey (and vinegar if desired) over the plants until fully submerged.
- Stir slowly to release air bubbles.
- Cover and let infuse for 2–3 weeks in a warm place, turning gently each day.
- Strain and store in a cool dark cupboard.

Properties: Detoxifying, lymphatic, mildly diuretic, gently uplifting.

Taste: Floral, bittersweet, with subtle green notes.

Energetics: Cooling, drying.

Uses: Supports spring cleansing, skin clarity, and lymph flow.

Solace Elixir

Ingredients

- Equal parts hawthorn berries, wild rose petals, and lemon balm
- Raw honey to cover
- Apple cider vinegar (optional, to preserve)

Instructions

- Fill a clean jar with herbs, cover with honey and apple cider vinegar.
- Infuse for 3–4 weeks, strain, and store in a dark place.

Properties: Cardiotonic, calming, mood-lifting.

Taste: Sweet, floral, gently citrus.

Energetics: Warming, moistening.

Uses: Supports heart function, eases anxiety, and nurtures emotional resilience.

SHRUBS & SPRITZERS

Wildflower Lemonade Shrub

Ingredients

- Juice of 3 lemons
- 2 tablespoons honey
- 1 tablespoon apple cider vinegar
- 1 teaspoon dried wild rose petals
- 1 teaspoon pineapple weed blossoms
- 1 teaspoon red clover blossoms
- 3 cups cold water

Instructions

- Mix honey and vinegar with lemon juice until dissolved.
- Add herbs and cold water.
- Chill for 1 hour, then strain.

Properties: Cooling, anti-inflammatory, mildly nervine.

Taste: Floral-citrus, bright, and lightly sweet.

Energetics: Cooling, moistening.

Uses: Restores electrolytes, soothes nerves, and refreshes body and mind in warm weather.

Pine Needle & Orange Spritzer

Ingredients

- 2 tablespoons chopped pine needles
- 2 orange slices
- 1 teaspoon honey
- 2 cups sparkling water

Instructions

- Steep pine and orange in warm water for 10 minutes.
- Strain, chill, and mix with honey and sparkling water.

Properties: Vitamin C-rich, respiratory-supportive, mood-lifting.

Taste: Resinous, citrusy, effervescent.

Energetics: Cooling, moistening.

Uses: Invigorates breathing, refreshes circulation, and lifts the spirit after work or travel.

LATTES & ROASTED BREWS

Earthen Heart Brew

Ingredients

- 1 teaspoon roasted burdock root
- 1 teaspoon roasted purple avens root (Geum triflorum)
- 1 teaspoon roasted chicory root
- ½ teaspoon raw cacao powder
- 1 cup water
- ½ cup milk of choice (dairy or plant-based)
- 1 teaspoon honey or maple syrup
- Pinch of cinnamon (optional)

Instructions

- Combine roots and water in a small pot.
- Simmer for 15–20 minutes until rich and fragrant.
- Strain, then whisk in cacao, milk, and sweetener.
- Sprinkle with cinnamon before serving.

Properties: Blood-cleansing, liver-supportive, adaptogenic, grounding.

Taste: Deep, earthy, mildly bitter with soft chocolate undertones.

Energetics: Warming, drying.

Uses: Supports digestion and liver function, balances blood sugar and mood. A tonic for replenishing energy while nurturing the heart.

Roasted Dandelion & Chicory Latte

Ingredients

- 1 tablespoon roasted dandelion root
- 1 tablespoon roasted chicory root
- 1 cup water
- ½ cup milk of choice (dairy, oat, almond, etc.)
- 1 teaspoon honey or maple syrup
- Pinch of cinnamon

Instructions

- Simmer roasted roots in water for 10–15 minutes.
- Strain, then whisk in warm milk and honey.
- Sprinkle with cinnamon before serving.

Properties: Liver-supportive, digestive, grounding.

Taste: Rich, nutty, mildly bitter-sweet.

Energetics: Warming, drying.

Uses: Supports detoxification, balances blood sugar, and provides a caffeine-free lift that steadies the nerves.

Part Seven: Winter
Walking Through Winter

Winter asks us to stop.

Not because we're tired. Because the earth itself is teaching us something we can only learn in stillness. This is the season where everything we've been learning finally integrates. The seeds dream beneath snow. The roots strengthen in frozen ground. What looks like absence is actually the deepest presence.

We've walked through emergence, abundance, and soul restoration. Now we come to the season that holds it all. The alchemy of mind, body, and spirit finally becoming one.

The Alchemy

Winter is transformation on our own terms. We've been metamorphosing all year, and now we arrive at this: living in a permissive state. Not subservient, not subordinate, not endlessly giving ourselves away. Balanced. Permission to rest. Permission to receive. Permission to simply be.

This is ceremony. Not the complexity we've been taught to expect. The simple function of living in balance.

Prayerful doesn't mean perfect words. It means walking with respect. Mindful doesn't mean cleared thoughts. It means staying present with what we actually feel.

And then there's that voice that speaks beneath all the teachings, the one that says: "Never was there a time that I existed without you." Is that the higher self recognizing itself? Is that the heart knowing exactly where we've been and where we're going? Or is it the ancestors reminding us we've never been alone?

Winter asks us these questions because the asking itself transforms us. The caterpillar doesn't know it will become a butterfly. It just knows it's time to stop moving and let something deeper begin.

The Cocoon

We could all use permission to cocoon when we feel it coming. Before we break, before we burn out, before external forces demand it. Not abandoning our responsibilities. Setting fair boundaries: "I need to slow down and turn inward for a while. I'm still here, just quieter."

We'll all face that final cocoon eventually. The one we don't choose the timing for. Before then, we can practice the smaller ones. The voluntary transformations. The conscious choice to dissolve what no longer serves and rebuild according to who we're becoming.

Self-care isn't luxury or retreat. It's the ceremony of grounding ourselves within life so we don't have to leave it entirely. The practice of honoring boundaries so crisis doesn't have to teach us what quiet wisdom already whispered.

Tea that warms from the inside out. Reflection that reveals what needs releasing. Introspection that shows us who we're becoming. Inventory of what we've carried and what we can finally set down. Honoring what brought us here. Letting go of what can't come with us.

This is calling ourselves back home. The same work we've been practicing all year, now deepened by winter's quiet and the closeness of our ancestors. When we honor these boundaries, crisis doesn't have to be our teacher. We learn to recognize the signs earlier. The tightness in chest, the shorter temper, the exhaustion that sleep doesn't fix.

The Continuity

There's beauty in the time we spend staying the same. Staying connected to spirit, hearing our real laugh and real voice, being the steady presence our families recognize and trust.

Winter gives us permission to just be. Not always growing, not always changing, not always striving. The seasons don't apologize for their consistency. Winter returns every year with the same invitation to slow down and remember.

This is the teaching: transformation is important. So is reliability. Being someone your people can count on to show up, year after year, with the same warmth they've always known.

Winter Solstice: The Cycle Returns

Winter Solstice arrives. The longest night, the first day of winter. Solstices and equinoxes hold power, carry meaning in the ceremonies of our lives. This is when our ceremonies would traditionally begin, when we'd gather to mark the turning of the wheel.

Maybe it's not the longest night when we look into our own light. Things are never as dim when our inner light hasn't diminished. Even when someone's earth walk is done, their light only grows brighter. Shining through memories, teachings, the love and space they hold even when their chair sits empty.

We put out spirit plates for those no longer here. You're still part of this meal, still part of this family, still part of the ceremony. Your chair may be empty, but the space you held remains full. Your presence hasn't left. It's just changed form.

The teaching: The light doesn't go out. It just changes form.

Here's what makes Solstice sacred beyond grief and remembering:

More light is gradually coming back.

After the longest night, each day grows incrementally brighter. The darkness has reached its fullest expression, and now, slowly, steadily, inevitably, the light returns.

This is the cycle we teach our children and our grandchildren:

Emerge (Spring) → Abundance (Summer) → Reflection (Fall) → Growth through ceremony (Winter) → Emerge again

And again. And again.

The cycle doesn't break. The light always returns. The seeds always dream beneath the snow. Spring always follows winter, no matter how long the darkness feels.

This is what we pass down. Not just plant knowledge or language or stories. The bone-deep trust that cycles continue, that light returns, that what looks like ending is actually preparation for beginning.

The ceremonies continue. The cycles turn. The light always, always returns.

This is the ceremony of trust: knowing that even in the deepest dark, we carry our own illumination. And those we love who've walked on? They're not dimmed by death. They're freed to shine even brighter, lighting the path for those of us still walking.

Winter Solstice isn't just about surviving the longest night. It's about remembering we're part of something that doesn't end. A cycle that continues through us, through our children, through all the generations yet to come.

The Long Handshake

Winter is where we put our best hopes forward.

Best hope, like the long handshake, is the manifestation of well wishes we carry for ourselves, our loved ones, and community. Often we start with inventory. Throwing out what no longer serves us to make way for the gifts we have yet to receive.

The long handshake is that extra moment of connection. The knowing that if we miss you on the road, our best hopes travel with you. That's how we all grow. We know the work it takes just to show up. Responsibilities, bills, family, everything life throws your way. We honor that work, even when we can't see it, even when it goes unwitnessed.

As we learn to walk through the seasons, as winter teaches us to walk with deeper attunement, we send our best hopes forward. Not as empty gesture. As recognition that we're all carrying something, we're all making tracks through difficult terrain.

Heart to yours. Spirit to spirit.

May your winter be warm. May your household be full. May you rest well.

And when the first thaw comes, when Spring begins to stir beneath the snow, the circle will begin once more. In gratitude, in wonder, and in love.

Winter asks us to stop. To gather what we've learned through the turning of seasons and sit with it.

Self first, to take care of the rest.

This is the season of ceremony. Not complexity. Function. Not performance. Presence. Not presents. The gift of being here, now, together.

Winter is not absence. Winter is presence in its deepest form.

It is where seeds dream and stories ripen. Where the snow teaches patience and the long nights invite reflection. In stillness, we return to ourselves. In silence, we hear the voice of Creator.

And in the cocoon of winter's deep rest, we become who we were always meant to be.

Kiʔsuʔk Kyukyit, K̓ukun Makut

May your heart stay warm with kindness. May your spirit stay attuned to creation's voice. May the ancestors walk close. May your household be full, rested, and whole. **May you always hear the language of the plants.**

Epilogue: The Long Handshake

Walking and Walking and Walking

We thought we were writing a book about plants.

A lifetime of walking through seasons, learning names in languages that almost forgot themselves, gathering with children and elders, making medicine. We thought we'd finally "know enough" to share.

The long handshake is that extra moment of connection. The knowing that if we miss you on the road, our best hopes travel with you.

This spring, yellowbell emerged in a place we've walked a thousand times and taught us something new. Even we had to learn what we taught in this book. Grandma and Grumpa both crossed over in 2023. They still teach. How grief is just love transformed. Something we might have missed about a plant. Even just memory of their hugs, their songs, their presence.

We're still students.

And that's the medicine. Not mastering, but continuing. Not arriving, but walking.

What This Bundle Carries

You're holding a lifetime of gathering. Not just plant profiles or recipes. An invitation into relationship. With plants, with language, with the land, with each other, with what our children already remember.

Through ʔamakʼis Ktunaxa, from Montana to Revelstoke, we've tried to share what the plants taught us: healing isn't something we accomplish once. It's practice, season after season.

This manuscript holds plant profiles with their teachings. Four seasons of ceremony. Ktunaxa and Salish names reconnecting us to 10,000 years of relationship. Stories our ancestors whispered and our children will carry forward. Recognition that "too much" sensitivity is often ancestral gift.

Mostly, it carries an invitation to keep walking.

The Teaching We Didn't Expect

We started preserving knowledge. Documenting it, teaching it to those who'd forgotten.

The deeper teaching emerged slowly: the medicine isn't in mastering information, it's in continuing relationship.

Showing up season after season. Bringing children who become our teachers. Making grandmother's medicine and discovering something new. Speaking old names and feeling them wake something up.

Walking itself is the medicine.

Not walking TO somewhere or AWAY from something. Just walking the way seasons walk. Cyclically, continuously, trusting the return.

What Walking Together Looks Like

After Fall's letting go and Winter's depth, spring reminds us what all that releasing prepares us for: emergence into relationship.

Walking together looks like making tea with children and letting them pour. Gathering medicine and leaving offerings. Speaking plant names that remember us back. Recognizing sensitivity as gift, not disorder. Trusting "too much" is often exactly enough. Returning to the same place year after year, seeing it new.

The long handshake. Connection that doesn't end with releasing hands. It continues as presence, as memory, as relationship shaping everything after.

For Those Who Cannot, Those Just Remembering, Those Yet to Come

Those who cannot walk these lands, speak these languages, gather these medicines. The teachings travel through these pages to meet you where you are. Distance doesn't break what relationship creates. You belong to this knowledge as much as anyone whose hands touch this soil.

Those just remembering. Waking to what grandmothers knew, what your body kept when your mind forgot, what your children already know. Trust what's stirring. Your ancestors are cheering from the other side. That "coming home" feeling? It's real. It's recognition. Welcome back, beloved.

Those yet to come. Our children, grandchildren, ones not yet born who'll walk these lands long after we're gone. You're why we do this. Every plant name we speak, we're speaking into your future. Every story we tell, we're remembering for you. You are loved now. You are remembered now. The teachings are already waiting for you to carry forward in your own way.

This is our covenant: for those who cannot, those just remembering, those yet to come.

The Transmission Works

This manuscript represents a lifetime of gathering. Years of recovery showing healing is possible. Years of watching Ayla learn what we're still learning.

Here's what we know: the transmission works.

Ayla identifies plants we've walked past for years. She speaks Ktunaxa words we're learning together. She gathers with attention we're all still practicing. The teachings don't stop when the teachers cross over. They move through us into her, and through her into the ones yet to come.

We're not the source. We're the middle of the story. Carrying what was handed to us. Adding what the plants taught us. Passing it to Ayla's generation.

That's how transmission works. We honor who taught us by trusting our children to carry it forward.

The Heart Space

We've walked through four seasons together. Emergence. Abundance. Reflection. Transformation.

Now we stand in the space between.

This is where we speak to those who taught us. Those who loved us into being. Those who crossed over before we were ready.

Grandma. Grandpa. Yours too.

When we miss them, when it catches us off guard, Ayla reminds us: "They can hear you when you say I love you. Remember, they're always around. If you miss them you can just talk to them."

So we do. In prayers. In quiet moments. In the way we raise her. In the medicine we make with our hands.

Take a moment. Name yours. Thank whoever loved you into being. Miss them. Love them.

The heart space has no walls. Everyone fits.

Keep Walking

Spring is already preparing next year's teachings. The cycle doesn't wait.

It just returns.

Walk your own land. Learn the names. Gather with respect. Bring your children. Make medicine. Speak the old languages. Trust the cycle.

Keep walking, season after season.

See You Next Spring

The long handshake continues. The transmission continues. The circle widens.

Not because we mastered anything. Because walking itself is medicine.

Come walk with us.

Spring returns. So do we. And so will you.

Hu sukiłqukni & čnes lemti

—Darcy & Jenny Fisher Keepers of the Seasons

The plants are still teaching. Ayla is still learning. The ancestors are still guiding. The circle never ends.

References

Introductory Note

Note: The following references were consulted to confirm plant taxonomy, Latin binomials, and regional range consistency across the territories where this work was conducted: Montana, Southeast British Columbia, the West Kootenays, Idaho, and north to Revelstoke. Each source was cross-referenced against teachings passed down through our family, elders, and community, and grounded in lived, land-based experience throughout ʔamakʼis Ktunaxa (Ktunaxa Land) and surrounding traditional territories. **These references were used for verification, not as the primary source of knowledge.**

Regarding Oral Tradition: The primary knowledge in this manuscript comes from oral teachings, family practice, and direct relationship with plants and land. While academic conventions require citation of published sources, we acknowledge that oral tradition cannot be reduced to citation formats designed for written texts. The teachings of Clark Matt, túpyeʔ (Genevieve Matt), David Raymond Williams, Wilfred Jacobs, Wilhelmenia "Willy" Wright, and other knowledge holders are cited as primary sources to honor their contributions, even as we recognize that their knowledge transcends conventional bibliographic representation. Ancestral plant knowledge transmitted through Jenny Fisher's family line (including Minnie Rittel and Marybelle Smith) is also honored, alongside the many medicine people and mentors whose teachings have shaped this work.

Regarding Ancestral Guidance: Leo Conrad Williams (grandfather to Darcy Fisher) visited in dream to inspire the writing of "Ka Papa" (Whitebark Pine teaching). This represents the continuation of knowledge transmission beyond the physical world, honoring the role of ancestors in guiding this work.

Regarding Traditional Stories: The traditional stories in this manuscript (Red Flower Girl, Kaʼs kiʼin numa, Ka Papa) represent Darcy Fisher's documented tellings, informed by teachings received from knowledge holders and lived experience on ʔamakʼis Ktunaxa. These are not historical recreations but living stories transmitted through practice and relationship.

Regarding Heritage & Knowledge Transmission: Darcy Fisher carries Ktunaxa heritage and is a member of the Ktunaxa Nation. Jenny Fisher carries Salish, Kootenai, and Pend d'Oreille blood. The knowledge in this manuscript reflects the convergence of these lineages through family teaching, lived experience, and direct relationship with the land and plants across traditional territories spanning Montana, Southeast British Columbia (including the West Kootenays), Idaho, and north to Revelstoke—the full range of ʔamaḱis Ktunaxa.

Regarding Retrieval Dates: Per APA 7th Edition guidelines, retrieval dates are included only for sources that are likely to change over time (such as wikis or databases with frequently updated content). For stable web pages and archived content, retrieval dates are omitted. Where included, dates reflect the period of active research for this manuscript (2023-2025).

Section 1 — Primary Sources & Teachings

Fisher, D., & Fisher, J. (2025). *Walking Through the Seasons: Teachings from ʔamaḱis Ktunaxa*. Keepers of the Seasons Publishing.

Fisher, D., & Fisher, J. (2023). *Keepers of the Seasons: Indigenous Connectedness and Land-Based Learning Workshops* [Workshop series]. Keepers of the Seasons, LLC.

Fisher, D., & Fisher, J. (in preparation). *The Living Apothecary: Nourishment and Medicine Through the Seasons*. Keepers of the Seasons Publishing.

Language Authorities:

Fisher, D. (2025). Ktunaxa language consultant and speaker [Personal knowledge]. Ktunaxa Nation member, ʔamaḱis Ktunaxa.

Fisher, J. (2025). Salish (Séliš), Kutenai, and Pend d'Oreille language consultant and speaker [Personal knowledge]. Salish, Kootenai, and Pend d'Oreille heritage.

Primary Knowledge Holders & Teachers:

Matt, C. (n.d.). Plant knowledge and traditional teachings [Oral teachings]. ʔamaḱis Ktunaxa territory.

Matt, G. "Jenny" (túpyeʔ). (d. 2023). Plant medicine, preservation, and traditional teachings [Oral teachings]. Salish, Kootenai, and Pend d'Oreille knowledge keeper.

Wright, W. "Willy". (n.d.). Traditional plant knowledge, stories, and medicine teachings [Oral teachings]. Jenny Fisher's aunt; sister to Clark Matt and Genevieve Matt.

Rittel, M. (n.d.). Ancestral plant knowledge [Oral teachings]. As transmitted through Jenny Fisher's family line.

Smith, M. (n.d.). Ancestral plant knowledge [Oral teachings]. As transmitted through Jenny Fisher's family line

Williams, D. R. (d. 2023). Plant knowledge and Ktunaxa language teachings [Oral teachings]. As transmitted to D. Fisher.

Williams, L. C. (d. n.d.). Ancestral teachings and spiritual guidance [Dream visitation]. Grandfather to D. Fisher; inspired the writing of "Ka Papa" (Whitebark Pine teaching).

Jacobs, W. (n.d.). Traditional plant knowledge and stories [Oral teachings]. Ktunaxa Nation.

Additional Mentors & Medicine People:

The authors gratefully acknowledge the many medicine people, teachers, and mentors whose generous sharing of knowledge, ceremony, and lived experience has shaped this work. While not individually cited throughout the manuscript, their teachings are woven into our understanding and practice. Out of respect for the depth and breadth of knowledge shared by numerous teachers across our journey, we honor their contributions collectively while recognizing that oral tradition and medicine teachings extend far beyond what can be captured in conventional citation formats.

Traditional Stories (as documented by authors):

Fisher, D. (2025). Red Flower Girl [Traditional story]. In *Walking Through the Seasons: Teachings from ʔamakis Ktunaxa*. Keepers of the Seasons Publishing.

Fisher, D. (2025). Kaʼs kiʼin numa (Thunder and the Old Woman) [Traditional Ktunaxa story]. In *Walking Through the Seasons: Teachings from ʔamakis Ktunaxa*. Keepers of the Seasons Publishing.

Fisher, D. (2025). Ka Papa [Traditional teaching stories]. In *Walking Through the Seasons: Teachings from ʔamakis Ktunaxa*. Keepers of the Seasons Publishing.

Note: Traditional teachings from Clark Matt, túpyeʔ (Genevieve Matt), David Raymond Williams, and Wilfred Jacobs were transmitted through oral tradition, family practice, and land-based learning. These teachings form the foundation of plant knowledge documented in this manuscript and are cited throughout as primary sources alongside the authors' direct experience. Traditional stories documented in this manuscript represent Darcy Fisher's tellings, informed by teachings received from knowledge holders and lived experience on ʔamakis Ktunaxa.

Section 2 — Verification Sources by Plant
Indigenous Knowledge & Language Resources

Confederated Salish and Kootenai Tribes. (n.d.). Salish Pend d'Oreille language reference guide. Retrieved from http://www.csktsalish.org/index.php/audio/salish-pend-d-oreille-language-reference-guide

FirstVoices. (n.d.). Ktunaxa dictionary. Retrieved from https://www.firstvoices.com/ktunaxa

Ktunaxa/Kinbasket Tribal Council. (1999). ʔa·kxam̓is q̓api qapsin' (All Living Things): A Ktunaxa Ethnobotany Handbook – Part One. Researched and compiled by Peter McCoy & Michael Keefer. Draft layout by Troy Hunter; final layout by Nicole Pawlak, Peter McCoy, & Michael Keefer. Ktunaxa/Kinbasket Tribal Council.

Montana Indian Nations Sacred Plant Guide. (2023). Rocky Mountain Tribal Leaders Council. Retrieved from https://www.rmtlc.org/wp-content/uploads/2023/11/MT_Indian_Nations_Sacred_Plants_Guide__Web.pdf

Turner, N. J., Kuhnlein, H. V., & Egger, K. N. (1987). The cottonwood mushroom (Tricholoma populinum Lange): A food resource of the Interior Salish Indian peoples of British Columbia. Canadian Journal of Botany, 65(5), 921–927.

Note: Language resources cited above are used for verification of spelling and linguistic consistency. Primary Salish language knowledge comes from Jenny Fisher's heritage and family transmission, not institutional affiliation. The ʔa·kxam̓is q̓api qapsin' handbook represents important documented Ktunaxa plant knowledge from the Ktunaxa/Kinbasket Tribal Council.

Turner, N. J., Thompson, L. C., Thompson, M. T., & York, A. Z. (1990). Thompson ethnobotany: Knowledge and usage of plants by the Thompson Indians of British Columbia. Royal British Columbia Museum.

Botanical & Taxonomic References

Burke Herbarium Image Collection. (n.d.). University of Washington. Retrieved from https://burkeherbarium.org/imagecollection/

Flora of North America Editorial Committee. (1993+). *Flora of North America North of Mexico* (Vol. 1+). Oxford University Press. http://www.efloras.org/flora_page.aspx?flora_id=1

Hitchcock, C. L., & Cronquist, A. (2018). *Flora of the Pacific Northwest: An illustrated manual* (2nd ed.). University of Washington Press.

Plants For A Future (PFAF). (n.d.). *Plants database*. Retrieved from https://pfaf.org

USDA, NRCS. (2025). *The PLANTS Database*. National Plant Data Team, Greensboro, NC. http://plants.usda.gov

Regional Field Guides & Conservation Resources

B.C. Conservation Data Centre. (2025). *Species summaries*. British Columbia Ministry of Environment. Retrieved from https://a100.gov.bc.ca/pub/eswp/

Montana Field Guide. (2025). Montana Natural Heritage Program and Montana Fish, Wildlife & Parks. Retrieved from https://fieldguide.mt.gov

NatureServe Explorer. (2025). *NatureServe conservation status*. Retrieved from https://explorer.natureserve.org

U.S. Forest Service & Federal Resources

USDA Forest Service. (n.d.). *Fire Effects Information System (FEIS)*. Rocky Mountain Research Station, Fire Sciences Laboratory. Retrieved from https://www.fs.usda.gov/database/feis/

U.S. National Park Service. (n.d.). *Native American ethnobotany database*. Retrieved from https://www.nps.gov/

Ethnobotanical & Traditional Use References

Moerman, D. E. (2010). Native American food plants: An ethnobotanical dictionary. Timber Press.

Moerman, D. E. (2010). Native American medicinal plants: An ethnobotanical dictionary. Timber Press.

Teit, J. A. (1930). The Salishan tribes of the western plateaus. Bureau of American Ethnology Annual Report 45. Smithsonian Institution.

Herbal Medicine & Phytochemistry References

Chevallier, A. (2016). *Encyclopedia of herbal medicine* (3rd ed.). DK Publishing.

Grieve, M. (1971). *A modern herbal* (Vols. 1–2). Dover Publications. (Original work published 1931)

Hoffmann, D. (2003). *Medical herbalism: The science principles and practices of herbal medicine*. Healing Arts Press.

Mills, S., & Bone, K. (2020). *Principles and practice of phytotherapy: Modern herbal medicine* (3rd ed.). Churchill Livingstone.

Online Databases & Citizen Science

iNaturalist. (n.d.). *Biodiversity observation network*. California Academy of Sciences & National Geographic Society. Retrieved from https://www.inaturalist.org

Calflora. (n.d.). *Information on California plants for education, research and conservation*. Retrieved from https://www.calflora.org

E-Flora BC. (n.d.). *Electronic atlas of the plants of British Columbia.* University of British Columbia. Retrieved from https://linnet.geog.ubc.ca/Atlas/Atlas.aspx?sciname=

Health & Nutritional Information

Healthline. (n.d.). *Nutrition and health information.* Retrieved from https://www.healthline.com

WebMD. (n.d.). *Vitamins and supplements.* Retrieved from https://www.webmd.com/vitamins/

Section 3 — Plant-Specific Verification Sources

The following sources were consulted for specific plants documented in this manuscript. Sources are organized alphabetically by plant common name.

Arnica (Heart-leafed Arnica, Arnica cordifolia)

B.C. Native Seed Manual. (n.d.). *Arnica cordifolia* Hook. British Columbia Ministry of Forests. Retrieved from https://www.env.gov.bc.ca/fia/documents/native_seed_manual/29arnica_cordifolia.pdf

Montana Field Guide. (2025). *Heart-leaf arnica – Arnica cordifolia.* Retrieved from https://fieldguide.mt.gov

USDA Forest Service. (n.d.). *Arnica cordifolia.* Fire Effects Information System. Retrieved from https://www.fs.usda.gov/database/feis/plants/forb/arccor/all.html

Balsamroot (Arrowleaf Balsamroot, *Balsamorhiza sagittata*)

Botanicheals. (2024). *Arrowleaf balsamroot medicinal uses.* Retrieved from https://botanicheals.com/arrowleaf-balsamroot-medicinal-uses/

Burke Herbarium Image Collection. (n.d.). *Balsamorhiza sagittata.* Retrieved from https://burkeherbarium.org/imagecollection/taxon.php?Taxon=Balsamorhiza+sagittata

Montana Field Guide. (2025). *Arrowleaf balsamroot – Balsamorhiza sagittata.* Retrieved from https://fieldguide.mt.gov

USDA Forest Service. (n.d.). *Balsamorhiza sagittata.* Fire Effects Information System. Retrieved from https://www.fs.usda.gov/database/feis/plants/forb/balsag/all.html

Bear Root (*Ligusticum canbyi*)

Burke Herbarium Image Collection. (n.d.). *Ligusticum canbyi.* Retrieved from https://burkeherbarium.org/imagecollection/taxon.php?Taxon=Ligusticum+canbyi

E-Flora BC. (n.d.). *Ligusticum canbyi.* Retrieved from https://linnet.geog.ubc.ca/Atlas/Atlas.aspx?sciname=Ligusticum+canbyi

Bearberry (Kinnikinnick, *Arctostaphylos uva-ursi*)

DrAxe. (n.d.). *Uva ursi (bearberry) benefits, uses, side effects.* Retrieved from https://draxe.com/nutrition/uva-ursi/

Montana Field Guide. (2025). *Kinnikinnick – Arctostaphylos uva-ursi.* Retrieved from https://fieldguide.mt.gov

USDA Forest Service. (n.d.). *Arctostaphylos uva-ursi.* Fire Effects Information System. Retrieved from https://www.fs.usda.gov/database/feis/plants/shrub/arcuva/all.html

Beargrass (*Xerophyllum tenax*)

Burke Herbarium Image Collection. (n.d.). *Xerophyllum tenax.* Retrieved from https://burkeherbarium.org/imagecollection/taxon.php?Taxon=Xerophyllum+tenax

University of Washington. (2008). *Xerophyllum tenax* propagation protocol. ESRM 412 Plant Production. Retrieved from https://courses.washington.edu/esrm412/protocols/2008/XETE.pdf

USDA Forest Service. (n.d.). *Xerophyllum tenax.* Retrieved from https://www.fs.usda.gov/wildflowers/plant-of-the-week/xerophyllum_tenax.shtml

Bergamot (Wild Bergamot, *Monarda fistulosa*)

Acorn Herbschool. (n.d.). *Wild bergamot – Monarda fistulosa.* Retrieved from https://acornherbschool.com/wild-bergamot/

Government of Manitoba. (n.d.). *Wild bergamot, bee balm, monarda.* Retrieved from https://www.gov.mb.ca/agriculture/crops/crop-management/bee-balm.html

Montana Field Guide. (2025). *Wild bergamot – Monarda fistulosa.* Retrieved from https://fieldguide.mt.gov

Bitterroot (*Lewisia rediviva*)

Burke Herbarium Image Collection. (n.d.). *Lewisia rediviva.* Retrieved from https://burkeherbarium.org/imagecollection/taxon.php?Taxon=Lewisia+rediviva

Montana Field Guide. (2025). *Bitterroot – Lewisia rediviva.* Retrieved from https://fieldguide.mt.gov/speciesDetail.aspx?elcode=PDPOR01010

USDA Forest Service. (n.d.). *Lewisia rediviva.* Fire Effects Information System. Retrieved from https://www.fs.usda.gov/database/feis/plants/forb/lewred/all.html

Bunchberry (*Cornus canadensis*)

ERA Library, University of Alberta. (n.d.). *Cornus canadensis.* Retrieved from https://era.library.ualberta.ca/items/e39a601a-fe02-4a4d-a3ba-d1eb8f7b83fe

Montana Field Guide. (2025). *Bunchberry dogwood – Cornus canadensis.* Retrieved from https://fieldguide.mt.gov/speciesDetail.aspx?elcode=pdcor01040

Native Plant Trust – Go Botany. (n.d.). *Bunchberry, Chamaepericlymenum canadense.* Retrieved from https://plantfinder.nativeplanttrust.org/plant/Chamaepericlymenum-canadense

USDA Forest Service. (n.d.). *Cornus canadensis.* Fire Effects Information System. Retrieved from https://www.fs.usda.gov/database/feis/plants/forb/corcan/all.html

Camas (*Camassia quamash*)

Burke Herbarium Image Collection. (n.d.). *Camassia quamash.* Retrieved from https://burkeherbarium.org/imagecollection/taxon.php?Taxon=Camassia+quamash

Montana Field Guide. (2025). *Common camas – Camassia quamash.* Retrieved from https://fieldguide.mt.gov

Plants For A Future. (n.d.). *Camassia quamash.* Retrieved from https://pfaf.org/user/Plant.aspx?LatinName=Camassia+quamash

Chokecherry (*Prunus virginiana*)

Native Memory Project. (2023, October 16). Chokecherry. Retrieved from https://nativememoryproject.org/plant/chokecherry/

Nowak, D., & Gołba, M. (2020). Antioxidant Content of Frozen, Convective Air-Dried, Freeze-Dried, and Infrared-Dried Chokecherry Fruits (Prunus virginiana L.). Plants, 9(3), 389. https://pmc.ncbi.nlm.nih.gov/articles/PMC7179396/

USDA Natural Resources Conservation Service. (n.d.). Plant Fact Sheet: Chokecherry (Prunus virginiana). Retrieved from https://plants.usda.gov/DocumentLibrary/factsheet/pdf/fs_prvi.pdf

Cedar (Western Red Cedar, *Thuja plicata*)

Burke Herbarium Image Collection. (n.d.). *Thuja plicata.* Retrieved from https://burkeherbarium.org/imagecollection/taxon.php?Taxon=Thuja+plicata

Montana Naturalist. (n.d.). *Culturally modified trees & cedar bark baskets.* Retrieved from https://montananaturalist.org

Silvics of British Columbia. (n.d.). *Western redcedar – Thuja plicata.* Government of British Columbia. Retrieved from https://www2.gov.bc.ca/assets/gov/farming-natural-resources-and-industry/forestry/silviculture/tree-species-selection/silvics_cw.pdf

USDA Forest Service. (n.d.). *Thuja plicata.* Retrieved from https://www.fs.usda.gov/database/feis/plants/tree/thupli/all.html

Dandelion (*Taraxacum officinale*)

Healthline. (n.d.). *Dandelion benefits*. Retrieved from https://www.healthline.com/nutrition/dandelion-benefits

Montana Field Guide. (2025). *Common dandelion – Taraxacum officinale*. Retrieved from https://fieldguide.mt.gov

USDA Forest Service. (n.d.). *Taraxacum officinale*. Fire Effects Information System. Retrieved from https://www.fs.usda.gov/database/feis/plants/forb/taroff/all.html

Devil's Club (*Oplopanax horridus*)

Burke Herbarium Image Collection. (n.d.). *Oplopanax horridus*. Retrieved from https://burkeherbarium.org/imagecollection/taxon.php?Taxon=Oplopanax+horridus

Montana Field Guide. (2025). *Devil's club – Oplopanax horridus*. Retrieved from https://fieldguide.mt.gov

USDA Forest Service. (n.d.). *Oplopanax horridus*. Fire Effects Information System. Retrieved from https://www.fs.usda.gov/database/feis/plants/shrub/oplhor/all.html

Elderberry (Blue Elderberry, *Sambucus cerulea*)

Boiron USA. (n.d.). *Nature's medicine chest: A look at elderberry*. Retrieved from https://www.boironusa.com/a-look-at-homeopathic-elderberry-sambucus/

USDA Forest Service. (n.d.). *Sambucus nigra* subsp. *cerulea*. Fire Effects Information System. Retrieved from https://www.fs.usda.gov/database/feis/plants/shrub/samnigc/all.html

WebMD. (n.d.). *Elderberry: Health benefits, risks, uses*. Retrieved from https://www.webmd.com/diet/elderberry-health-benefits

Fireweed (*Chamaenerion angustifolium*)

Montana Field Guide. (2025). *Fireweed – Chamaenerion angustifolium*. Retrieved from https://fieldguide.mt.gov

Native Plant Trust. (n.d.). *Fireweed, Chamerion angustifolium*. Retrieved from https://plantfinder.nativeplanttrust.org/plant/Chamaenerion-angustifolium

USDA Forest Service. (n.d.). *Chamaenerion angustifolium*. Fire Effects Information System. Retrieved from https://www.fs.usda.gov/database/feis/plants/forb/chaang/all.html

Glacier Lily (*Erythronium grandiflorum*)

Burke Herbarium Image Collection. (n.d.). *Erythronium grandiflorum*. Retrieved from https://burkeherbarium.org/imagecollection/taxon.php?Taxon=Erythronium+grandiflorum

Montana Field Guide. (2025). *Yellow avalanche lily – Erythronium grandiflorum*. Retrieved from https://fieldguide.mt.gov

USDA Forest Service. (n.d.). *Yellow avalanche-lily (Erythronium grandiflorum)*. Retrieved from https://www.fs.usda.gov/wildflowers/beauty/avalanche_lilies/erythronium_grandiflorum.shtml

Horsehair Lichen (*Bryoria fremontii*)

Montana Field Guide. (2025). *Fremont's horsehair lichen – Bryoria fremontii*. Retrieved from https://fieldguide.mt.gov

USDA Forest Service. (n.d.). *Bryoria fremontii*. Retrieved from https://www.fs.usda.gov/

Huckleberry (*Vaccinium* spp.)

DrAxe. (n.d.). Huckleberries: Benefits, nutrition & recipes. Retrieved from https://draxe.com/nutrition/huckleberries/

Montana Field Guide. (2025). Common huckleberry – Vaccinium membranaceum. Retrieved from https://fieldguide.mt.gov

Northwest Wild Foods. (n.d.). Huckleberry nutrition and health benefits. Retrieved from https://nwwildfoods.com

USDA Forest Service. (n.d.). Vaccinium species. Fire Effects Information System. Retrieved from https://www.fs.usda.gov/database/feis/

Juniper (Rocky Mountain Juniper, *Juniperus scopulorum*)

Montana Field Guide. (2025). *Rocky Mountain juniper – Juniperus scopulorum*. Retrieved from https://fieldguide.mt.gov

USDA Forest Service. (n.d.). *Juniperus scopulorum*. Retrieved from https://www.fs.usda.gov/database/feis/plants/tree/junsco/all.html

USDA PLANTS. (n.d.). *Rocky Mountain juniper plant guide*. Retrieved from https://plants.usda.gov/DocumentLibrary/plantguide/pdf/pg_jusc2.pdf

Kinnikinnick (see Bearberry)

Labrador Tea (*Rhododendron groenlandicum*)

Burke Herbarium Image Collection. (n.d.). *Rhododendron groenlandicum*. Retrieved from https://burkeherbarium.org/imagecollection/taxon.php?Taxon=Rhododendron+groenlandicum

Montana Field Guide. (2025). *Labrador tea – Rhododendron groenlandicum*. Retrieved from https://fieldguide.mt.gov

Lady's Slipper Orchids (*Cypripedium* spp.)

Alaska Center for Conservation Science. (n.d.). *Cypripedium montanum* (mountain lady's slipper) assessment. Retrieved from https://accs.uaa.alaska.edu/wp-content/uploads/Cypripedium-montanum_Assessment_Final.pdf

Burke Herbarium Image Collection. (n.d.). *Calypso bulbosa*. Retrieved from https://burkeherbarium.org/imagecollection/taxon.php?Taxon=Calypso+bulbosa

USDA Forest Service. (n.d.). *Cypripedium montanum – The slipper orchids*. Retrieved from https://www.fs.usda.gov/wildflowers/beauty/cypripediums/cypripedium_montanum.shtml

Northern Bedstraw (*Galium boreale*)

Alberta Conservation & Reclamation Research on Ecological Services. (n.d.). *Galium boreale*. University of Alberta. Retrieved from https://acrre.ualberta.ca/

NatureGate. (n.d.). *Northern bedstraw, Galium boreale*. Retrieved from https://luontoportti.com/en/t/1055

Plants For A Future. (n.d.). *Galium boreale*. Retrieved from https://pfaf.org/user/Plant.aspx?LatinName=Galium+boreale

Nodding Onion (*Allium cernuum*)

Wisconsin Horticulture. (n.d.). Nodding onion, Allium cernuum. University of Wisconsin-Madison Extension. Retrieved from https://hort.extension.wisc.edu/articles/nodding-onion-allium-cernuum/

Montana Field Guide. (2025). Nodding onion – Allium cernuum. Retrieved from https://fieldguide.mt.gov

Pineapple Weed (*Matricaria discoidea*)

Burke Herbarium Image Collection. (n.d.). *Matricaria discoidea*. Retrieved from https://burkeherbarium.org/imagecollection/taxon.php?Taxon=Matricaria+discoidea

Montana Plant Life. (n.d.). *Matricaria discoidea*. Retrieved from http://montana.plant-life.org/

Prickly Pear (*Opuntia fragilis*)

Drugs.com. (n.d.). Prickly pear uses, benefits & dosage. Retrieved from https://www.drugs.com/npp/prickly-pear.html

Montana Field Guide. (2025). Brittle pricklypear – Opuntia fragilis. Retrieved from https://fieldguide.mt.gov

Red Clover (*Trifolium pratense*)

Healthline. (n.d.). *Red clover*. Retrieved from https://www.healthline.com/nutrition/red-clover

WebMD. (n.d.). *Red clover*. Retrieved from https://www.webmd.com/vitamins/ai/ingredientmono-308/red-clover

Rose (Wood's Rose, *Rosa woodsii*)

Burke Herbarium Image Collection. (n.d.). *Rosa woodsii*. Retrieved from https://burkeherbarium.org/imagecollection/taxon.php?Taxon=Rosa+woodsii

Montana Field Guide. (2025). *Woods' rose – Rosa woodsii*. Retrieved from https://fieldguide.mt.gov

Southwest Desert Flora. (n.d.). *Rosa woodsii, Woods rose*. Retrieved from http://southwestdesertflora.com/WebsiteFolders/All_Species/Rosaceae/Rosa%20woodsii,%20Woods%20Rose.html

USDA Forest Service. (n.d.). *Rosa woodsii*. Fire Effects Information System. Retrieved from https://www.fs.usda.gov/database/feis/plants/shrub/roswoo/all.html

Saskatoon (Serviceberry, *Amelanchier alnifolia*)

American Indian Health and Diet Project. (n.d.). Serviceberry. University of Kansas. Retrieved from https://aihd.ku.edu/foods/serviceberry.html

Montana Field Guide. (2025). Saskatoon serviceberry – Amelanchier alnifolia. Retrieved from https://fieldguide.mt.gov

Native Plants PNW. (n.d.). Saskatoon serviceberry, Amelanchier alnifolia. Retrieved from https://nativeplantspnw.com/saskatoon-serviceberry-amelanchier-alnifolia/

USDA Forest Service. (n.d.). Amelanchier alnifolia. Fire Effects Information System. Retrieved from https://www.fs.usda.gov/database/feis/plants/shrub/amealn/all.html

Skunk Cabbage (*Lysichiton americanus*)

Alaska Ethnobotany. (n.d.). *Western skunk cabbage pit roasted steelhead trout*. University of Alaska Fairbanks. Retrieved from https://alaskaethnobotany.community.uaf.edu/western-skunk-cabbage-pit-roasted-steelhead-trout/

B.C. Conservation Data Centre. (2025). *Species summary – Lysichiton americanus* skunk cabbage. Retrieved from https://a100.gov.bc.ca/pub/eswp/

Montana Field Guide. (2025). *American skunk-cabbage – Lysichiton americanus*. Retrieved from https://fieldguide.mt.gov

Sticky Purple Geranium (*Geranium viscosissimum*)

Burke Herbarium Image Collection. (n.d.). *Geranium viscosissimum*. Retrieved from https://burkeherbarium.org/imagecollection/taxon.php?Taxon=Geranium+viscosissimum

Montana Field Guide. (2025). *Sticky purple geranium – Geranium viscosissimum*. Retrieved from https://fieldguide.mt.gov

Thimbleberry (*Rubus parviflorus*)

Montana Field Guide. (2025). Thimbleberry – Rubus parviflorus. Retrieved from https://fieldguide.mt.gov

Native Plants PNW. (n.d.). Thimbleberry, Rubus parviflorus. Retrieved from https://nativeplantspnw.com/thimbleberry-rubus-parviflorus/

Trillium (*Trillium ovatum*)

Burke Herbarium Image Collection. (2024). *Trillium ovatum*. Retrieved from https://burkeherbarium.org/imagecollection/taxon.php?Taxon=Trillium+ovatum

Montana Field Guide. (2025). *Western trillium – Trillium ovatum*. Retrieved from https://fieldguide.mt.gov

USDA Forest Service. (n.d.). *Trilliums*. Retrieved from https://www.fs.usda.gov/wildflowers/beauty/trilliums/about.shtml

Violet (*Viola* spp.)

Go Botany. (n.d.). *Genus Viola*. Native Plant Trust. Retrieved from https://gobotany.nativeplanttrust.org/genus/viola/

Montana Field Guide. (2025). *Stream violet – Viola glabella*. Retrieved from https://fieldguide.mt.gov

Yarrow (*Achillea millefolium*)

Ayur Times. (n.d.). *Achillea millefolium (common yarrow) medicinal uses*. Retrieved from https://www.ayurtimes.com/achillea-millefolium/

Montana Field Guide. (2025). *Common yarrow – Achillea millefolium*. Retrieved from https://fieldguide.mt.gov/speciesDetail.aspx?elcode=PDAST01060

Alder (*Alnus* spp.)

Burke Herbarium Image Collection. (n.d.). *Alnus* species. Retrieved from https://burkeherbarium.org/imagecollection/browse.php?Genus=Alnus

Montana Field Guide. (2025). *Thinleaf alder – Alnus incana*. Retrieved from https://fieldguide.mt.gov

USDA Forest Service. (n.d.). *Alnus* species. Fire Effects Information System. Retrieved from https://www.fs.usda.gov/database/feis/

Burdock (Common Burdock, *Arctium minus*)

Healthline. (n.d.). *Burdock root*. Retrieved from https://www.healthline.com/health/burdock-root

Montana Field Guide. (2025). *Lesser burdock – Arctium minus*. Retrieved from https://fieldguide.mt.gov

WebMD. (n.d.). *Burdock root health benefits*. Retrieved from https://www.webmd.com/diet/health-benefits-burdock-root

Cottonwood (*Populus balsamifera / P. trichocarpa*)

Burke Herbarium Image Collection. (n.d.). *Populus balsamifera*. Retrieved from https://burkeherbarium.org/imagecollection/taxon.php?Taxon=Populus+balsamifera

Montana Field Guide. (2025). *Black cottonwood – Populus trichocarpa*. Retrieved from https://fieldguide.mt.gov

USDA Forest Service. (n.d.). *Populus balsamifera*. Fire Effects Information System. Retrieved from https://www.fs.usda.gov/database/feis/plants/tree/popbal/all.html

Dogbane (Creeping Dogbane, *Apocynum cannabinum*)

Burke Herbarium Image Collection. (n.d.). *Apocynum cannabinum*. Retrieved from https://burkeherbarium.org/imagecollection/taxon.php?Taxon=Apocynum+cannabinum

Montana Field Guide. (2025). *Indian hemp – Apocynum cannabinum*. Retrieved from https://fieldguide.mt.gov

Plants For A Future. (n.d.). *Apocynum cannabinum*. Retrieved from https://pfaf.org/user/Plant.aspx?LatinName=Apocynum+cannabinum

Evergreen Needles & Tree Resin (Various Conifers)

Montana Field Guide. (2025). *Conifer species of Montana*. Retrieved from https://fieldguide.mt.gov

USDA Forest Service. (n.d.). *Pine, spruce, and fir resin uses*. Retrieved from https://www.fs.usda.gov/

Lomatium (Nine-leaf Biscuitroot, *Lomatium triternatum*)

Burke Herbarium Image Collection. (n.d.). *Lomatium triternatum*. Retrieved from https://burkeherbarium.org/imagecollection/taxon.php?Taxon=Lomatium+triternatum

Montana Field Guide. (2025). *Nine-leaf desert-parsley – Lomatium triternatum*. Retrieved from https://fieldguide.mt.gov

Mullein (Great Mullein, *Verbascum thapsus*)

Montana Field Guide. (2025). Common mullein – Verbascum thapsus. Retrieved from https://fieldguide.mt.gov

USDA Forest Service. (n.d.). Verbascum thapsus. Fire Effects Information System. Retrieved from https://www.fs.usda.gov/database/feis/plants/forb/vertah/all.html

WebMD. (n.d.). Mullein tea health benefits. Retrieved from https://www.webmd.com/diet/health-benefits-mullein-tea

Pipsissewa (*Chimaphila umbellata*)

Burke Herbarium Image Collection. (n.d.). *Chimaphila umbellata*. Retrieved from https://burkeherbarium.org/imagecollection/taxon.php?Taxon=Chimaphila+umbellata

Montana Field Guide. (2025). *Prince's pine – Chimaphila umbellata*. Retrieved from https://fieldguide.mt.gov

Plants For A Future. (n.d.). *Chimaphila umbellata*. Retrieved from https://pfaf.org/user/Plant.aspx?LatinName=Chimaphila+umbellata

Prairie Crocus (*Anemone patens*)

Burke Herbarium Image Collection. (n.d.). *Anemone patens*. Retrieved from https://burkeherbarium.org/imagecollection/taxon.php?Taxon=Anemone+patens

Montana Field Guide. (2025). *Pasqueflower – Anemone patens*. Retrieved from https://fieldguide.mt.gov

Red-osier Dogwood (*Cornus sericea*)

Montana Field Guide. (2025). *Red-osier dogwood – Cornus sericea*. Retrieved from https://fieldguide.mt.gov

USDA Forest Service. (n.d.). *Cornus sericea*. Fire Effects Information System. Retrieved from https://www.fs.usda.gov/database/feis/plants/shrub/corser/all.html

Soapberry (Foamberry, *Shepherdia canadensis*)

Burke Herbarium Image Collection. (n.d.). *Shepherdia canadensis*. Retrieved from https://burkeherbarium.org/imagecollection/taxon.php?Taxon=Shepherdia+canadensis

Montana Field Guide. (2025). *Canada buffaloberry – Shepherdia canadensis*. Retrieved from https://fieldguide.mt.gov

USDA Forest Service. (n.d.). *Shepherdia canadensis*. Fire Effects Information System. Retrieved from https://www.fs.usda.gov/database/feis/plants/shrub/shecan/all.html

Spring Beauty (*Claytonia lanceolata*)

Burke Herbarium Image Collection. (n.d.). *Claytonia lanceolata*. Retrieved from https://burkeherbarium.org/imagecollection/taxon.php?Taxon=Claytonia+lanceolata

Montana Field Guide. (2025). *Western spring beauty – Claytonia lanceolata*. Retrieved from https://fieldguide.mt.gov

Plants For A Future. (n.d.). *Claytonia lanceolata*. Retrieved from https://pfaf.org/user/Plant.aspx?LatinName=Claytonia+lanceolata

Whitebark Pine (*Pinus albicaulis*)

Montana Field Guide. (2025). *Whitebark pine – Pinus albicaulis*. Retrieved from https://fieldguide.mt.gov/speciesDetail.

aspx?elcode=pgpin04010

U.S. Fish and Wildlife Service. (n.d.). *Whitebark pine (Pinus albicaulis)*. Retrieved from https://www.fws.gov/species/whitebark-pine-pinus-albicaulis

USDA Forest Service. (n.d.). *Pinus albicaulis*. Fire Effects Information System. Retrieved from https://www.fs.usda.gov/database/feis/plants/tree/pinalb/all.html

Wild Carrot (*Daucus carota*)

Montana Field Guide. (2025). Wild carrot – Daucus carota. Retrieved from https://fieldguide.mt.gov

Plants For A Future. (n.d.). Daucus carota. Retrieved from https://pfaf.org/user/Plant.aspx?LatinName=Daucus+carota

Wild Strawberry (*Fragaria virginiana*)

Burke Herbarium Image Collection. (n.d.). *Fragaria virginiana*. Retrieved from https://burkeherbarium.org/imagecollection/taxon.php?Taxon=Fragaria+virginiana

Montana Field Guide. (2025). *Virginia strawberry – Fragaria virginiana*. Retrieved from https://fieldguide.mt.gov

USDA Forest Service. (n.d.). *Fragaria virginiana*. Fire Effects Information System. Retrieved from https://www.fs.usda.gov/database/feis/plants/forb/fravir/all.html

Willow (*Salix* spp.)

Burke Herbarium Image Collection. (n.d.). *Salix* species. Retrieved from https://burkeherbarium.org/imagecollection/browse.php?Genus=Salix

Montana Field Guide. (2025). *Willow species*. Retrieved from https://fieldguide.mt.gov

USDA Forest Service. (n.d.). *Salix* species. Fire Effects Information System. Retrieved from https://www.fs.usda.gov/database/feis/

Yellowbells (*Fritillaria pudica*)

Burke Herbarium Image Collection. (n.d.). *Fritillaria pudica*. Retrieved from https://burkeherbarium.org/imagecollection/taxon.php?Taxon=Fritillaria+pudica

Montana Field Guide. (2025). *Yellow fritillary – Fritillaria pudica*. Retrieved from https://fieldguide.mt.gov

USDA Forest Service. (n.d.). *Fritillaria pudica*. Retrieved from https://www.fs.usda.gov/wildflowers/

Section 4 — Additional Web Resources Consulted

The following online resources were consulted for supplementary information on plant identification, traditional uses, and health properties. These sources provided verification of botanical details and contemporary applications.

Health & Wellness Databases

Drugs.com. (n.d.). *Natural medicines comprehensive database.* Retrieved from https://www.drugs.com/

Examine.com. (n.d.). *Nutrition and supplement research.* Retrieved from https://examine.com/

MedicineNet. (n.d.). *Vitamins and supplements.* Retrieved from https://www.medicinenet.com/

Herbal Reference Sites

Henriette's Herbal Homepage. (n.d.). Retrieved from https://henriettes-herb.com/

Mountain Rose Herbs. (n.d.). *Herbalism resources.* Retrieved from https://mountainroseherbs.com/

The Herbal Academy. (n.d.). *Herbal education.* Retrieved from https://theherbalacademy.com/

Regional Plant Guides

E-Flora BC. (n.d.). *Electronic atlas of the plants of British Columbia.* University of British Columbia. Retrieved from https://linnet.geog.ubc.ca/Atlas/Atlas.aspx

Montana Plant Life. (n.d.). *Montana plant species.* Retrieved from http://montana.plant-life.org/

Native Plants PNW. (n.d.). *Pacific Northwest native plant guide.* Retrieved from https://nativeplantspnw.com/

End of References

This bibliography represents verification sources consulted for "Walking Through the Seasons: Teachings from ʔamakis Ktunaxa" (2025). The primary knowledge contained in this manuscript comes from lived experience, family teachings, and direct relationship with the land and plants of ʔamakis Ktunaxa.

GLOSSARY

A

C

Ceremony - Not complexity, but function. The practice of living in right relationship with all living things; the simple act of being present with intention

Calling Ourselves Home - The practice of returning to wholeness, recognizing and reclaiming the parts of ourselves we've lost or given away

Decoction - A method of extracting medicine from roots, bark, or hard plant materials by simmering in water for an extended period

E

Elixir - A sweet medicinal preparation, often made with honey or glycerin, used for both healing and nourishment

Energetics - The warming, cooling, drying, or moistening qualities of plants and how they interact with the body's systems

F

Four Quadrants - A teaching framework for understanding wholeness and permission work: Physical, Mental, Emotional, Spiritual

G

Gratitude - One of the foundational principles; giving thanks not because we should, but because the plants can feel when we mean it

H

Humility - Staying humble enough to know when we're wrong; remaining students for life. The plants have been here longer than we have

I

Infusion - A method of extracting medicine by steeping plant material (usually leaves and flowers) in hot water

Integrity - Following through on what we promise, even when no one's watching. The plants know when our hearts match our words

K

Ka Papa (Ktunaxa) - My grandfather; also refers to teachings that combine what the grandfather knew with what the plants offer; medicine created through the synthesis of ancestral knowledge and direct plant relationship

kanuɫmaquɫaqpiʔk (Ktunaxa) - Cottonwood

kaɫmuxu (Ktunaxa) - Wild Strawberry

Kiʔsuʔk Kyukyit, Kukun Makut (Ktunaxa) - Traditional New Year greeting; a heart and spirit wish for those we love

kupaʔtiɫ (Ktunaxa) - Foamberry, Soapberry (Soopolallie)

M

Medicine - Not just plants that heal physical ailments, but anything that restores balance and right relationship—including food, ceremony, connection, and presence

mukwuʔk (Ktunaxa) - Red osier dogwood

N

naɫi·ȼaxawuʔk (Ktunaxa) - Devil's Club

naʔhik (Ktunaxa) - Picking baskets

Nasuʔkin (Ktunaxa) - Chief

nupika (Ktunaxa) - Ancestors, those who came before; Spirit; the ones whose footsteps are not behind us but beneath us

P

Permissive State - Living in balance; not subservient, not subordinate, not endlessly giving ourselves away. Permission to rest, receive, and simply be

Poultice - Fresh or moistened plant material applied directly to the skin for healing wounds, reducing inflammation, or drawing out infection

Properties - The medicinal actions of plants (antibacterial, anti-inflammatory, etc.)

Protocol - Setting intention with heart and mind connected; asking permission of the living being before harvest; leaving the land better than we found it

Q
qaɬukp (Ktunaxa) - Yellowbells

q̓uɬwa (Ktunaxa) - Roses

R
Reciprocity - Taking only what we need, leaving the rest; offering tobacco, song, something of personal value—not as payment, but as relationship. Everything is always giving; we learn to give back

S
Salve - A healing ointment made by infusing plant material in oil and thickening with beeswax or other natural solidifiers

Soul Restoration - The process of remembering and reclaiming wholeness; healing the distance between who we are and who we've been told to be

sq̓umu (Ktunaxa) - Serviceberry / Saskatoon Berry

sqepc (Salish) - Spring season

T
tu̓pyeʔ (Salish) - Great grandparent

tax niʔ pik̓ak (Ktunaxa) - A long time ago; traditional story opening

Tincture - A concentrated liquid extract of plant medicine, usually made with alcohol as the solvent

Tonic - A plant medicine taken regularly to support overall health and vitality rather than treat acute conditions

W
waʔta (Ktunaxa) - Spring Beauty, Indian Potato

X
xapi (Ktunaxa) - Camas

xaɬ (Ktunaxa) - Arrow leaf balsamroot

ɬ

ɬam̓ (Ktunaxa) - Willow

ɬawiyaɬ (Ktunaxa) - Huckleberry

ɬumayitnamu (Ktunaxa) - Spring season

ʔ

ʔa·kinmiɬumayit (Ktunaxa) - Spring season

ʔa·kɬukaqwum (Ktunaxa) - The Ktunaxa language; the living language that has evolved over 10,000 years of intimate relationship with the homeland

ʔa·knumuȼtiɬiɬ (Ktunaxa) - Natural Law and Order; the understanding that everything moves in relationship

ʔa·kpiȼis ɬawu (Ktunaxa) - "Elk's (cow's) favorite food"; Pipsissewa

ʔa·kxam̓is q̓api qapsin' (Ktunaxa) - All living things, all that exists

ʔakuɬwuʔk (Ktunaxa) - Alder

ʔakuwaɬ (Ktunaxa) - Nodding Onion

ʔa·kuwaɬwuʔk (Ktunaxa) - Birch Tree/Paper Birch

ʔa·kwuʔk̓ (Ktunaxa) - Bark removed from tree

ʔa·q̓uku / kaɬmuxu (Ktunaxa) - Wild Strawberry, Woodland Strawberry

ʔamak (Ktunaxa) - The land

ʔamak̓is Ktunaxa (Ktunaxa) - Ktunaxa Land, the homeland

ʔaɬa (Ktunaxa) - Edible Horsehair (lichen)

ʔawumu (Ktunaxa) - Medicine

ʔayut (Ktunaxa) - Bear Root; also refers to medicine or those who hold specific medicine

ʔinq̓um (Ktunaxa) - Skunk Cabbage

About the Authors

We are the founders of Keepers of the Seasons LLC, creators of Six Twenty Skincare, and developers of the Speaking Earth Education Network (S.E.E.N.). A land-based learning initiative that meets learners where they are through real life, real time experiential learning. S.E.E.N. honors sensitivity as ancestral gift rather than disorder, supporting people of all ages in reconnecting with plant wisdom and land-based knowledge.

We offer seasonal workshops, plant medicine education, and family-centered learning experiences. Our work centers lived relationship with plants and land, passed through generations and practiced daily.

We also work with organizations to develop curriculum, provide professional development, and deliver customized land-based learning programs.

The Walking Through the Seasons Trilogy guides readers from remembering to living, through food, plant relationship, and the everyday acts that connect body, land, and spirit:

Walking Through the Seasons: A Living Archive of Ceremony, Territory, and the Plants That Remember Us. The Remembering (Spirit and Story).

The Living Apothecary. The Living (Body and Practice).

Seasons of the Medicine Wheel. The Teaching (Community and Continuity).

We live in Montana with our children, who teach us daily that the transmission works. The old knowledge is already alive in the next generation.

Connect with us:

Visit www.sixtwenty.net to explore workshops, events, and organizational partnerships

Email: info@kotstek.com for curriculum development and professional development inquiries

Six Twenty Skincare: www.sixtwenty.net

www.ingramcontent.com/pod-product-compliance
Lightning Source LLC
Chambersburg PA
CBHW040934030426
42337CB00006B/53